REA's Flashcards™

SPANISH

Staff of Research and Education Association,
Dr. M. Fogiel, Director

Research & Education Association
61 Ethel Road West
Piscataway, New Jersey 08854

REA's INTERACTIVE FLASHCARDS™ SPANISH

Copyright © 1999 by Research & Education Association. All rights reserved. No part of this book may be reproduced in any form without permission of the publisher.

Printed in the United States of America

Library of Congress Catalog Card Number 98-67205

International Standard Book Number 0-87891-163-4

Research & Education Association, Piscataway, New Jersey 08854

REA's Interactive Flashcards
What they're for
How to use them

They come in a book, not in a box of hundreds of loose cards.

They are most useful as test time approaches to help you check your test readiness.

They are a good tool for self-study and also for group study. They can even be used as a competitive game to see who scores best.

They work with any text.

The interactive feature is a unique learning tool. With it, you can write in your own answer to each question which you can then check against the correct answer provided on the flip side of each card.

You will find that the flashcards in a book have several advantages over flashcards in a box.

You don't have to cope with hundreds of loose cards. Whenever you want to study, you don't have to decide beforehand which cards you are likely to need; you don't have to pull them out of a box (and later return them in their proper place). You can just open the book and get going without ado.

A very detailed index will guide you to whatever topics you want to cover.

A number of blank card pages is included, in case you want to construct some of your own Q's and A's.

You can take along REA's flashcard book anywhere, ready for use when you are. You don't need to tote along the box or a bunch of loose cards.

REA's Flashcard books have been carefully put together with REA's customary concern for quality. We believe you will find them an excellent review and study tool.

Dr. M. Fogiel
Program Director

P.S. As you could tell, you could see all the flashcards in the book while you were in the store; they aren't sealed in shrink-wrap.

HOW TO USE THE FLASHCARDS IN THIS BOOK

There are several types of questions that you will encounter in this book. They include fill-in-the blank questions and true-or-false questions.

In addition, you will encounter some questions in Spanish with a verb in parentheses that is also in Spanish. When you do, conjugate the verb. Here is an example:

Question:

Es evidente que (LLOVER) mañana.

Answer:

lloverá/va llover

In some other instances, you will find a sentence in Spanish and one or more words in parentheses in English. For those questions, the answer should be in Spanish. Here is an example:

Question:

Lo haré antes de que (THEY ARRIVE).

Answer:

LLEGUEN

Questions

Q1

What are the two past subjunctive forms for *quepamos*?

Your Own Answer_____

Q2

What are the two past subjunctive forms for *sea*?

Your Own Answer_____

Q3

What are the two past subjunctive forms for *digas*?

Your Own Answer_____

Correct Answers

A1

cupiéramos/cupiésemos

A2

fuera/fuese

A3

dijeras/dijeses

Questions

Q4

What are the two past subjunctive forms for *comiencen*?

*Your Own Answer*_____

Q5

What are the two past subjunctive forms for *escojan*?

*Your Own Answer*_____

Q6

What are the two past subjunctive forms for *huela*?

*Your Own Answer*_____

Correct Answers

A4

comenzaran/comenzasen

A5

escogieran/escogiesen

A6

oliera/oliese

Questions

Q7

What are the two past subjunctive forms for *traigas*?

*Your Own Answer*_____

Q8

What are the two past subjunctive forms for *elija*?

*Your Own Answer*_____

Q9

What are the two past subjunctive forms for *envíen*?

*Your Own Answer*_____

Correct Answers

A7

trajeras/trajeses

A8

eligiera/eligiese

A9

enviaran/enviasen

Questions

Q10

What are the two past subjunctive forms for *averigües*?

Your Own Answer_____

Q11

What are the two past subjunctive forms for *sepamos*?

Your Own Answer_____

Q12

What are the two past subjunctive forms for *sigas*?

Your Own Answer_____

Correct Answers

A10

averiguaras/averiguases

A11

supiéramos/supiésemos

A12

siguieras/siguieses

Questions

Q13

What are the two past subjunctive forms for *os divirtáis*?

Your Own Answer_____

Q14

What are the two past subjunctive forms for *ruegue*?

Your Own Answer_____

Q15

What are the two past subjunctive forms for *almuerces*?

Your Own Answer_____

Correct Answers

A13

os divirtierais/os divirtieseis

A14

rogara/rogase

A15

almorzaras/almorzases

Questions

Q16

What are the two past subjunctive forms for *deshuese*?

Your Own Answer_____

Q17

What are the two past subjunctive forms for *parezcan*?

Your Own Answer_____

Q18

What are the two past subjunctive forms for *se deslicen*?

Your Own Answer_____

Correct Answers

A16

deshuesara/deshuesase

A17

parecieran/pareciesen

A18

se deslizaran/se deslizasen

Questions

Q19

What are the two past subjunctive forms for *convenzas*?

*Your Own Answer*____

Q20

What are the two past subjunctive forms for *recojas*?

*Your Own Answer*____

Q21

What are the two past subjunctive forms for *agregue*?

*Your Own Answer*____

Correct Answers

A19

convencieras/convencieses

A20

recogiera/recogiese

A21

agregara/agregase

Questions

Q22

What are the two past subjunctive forms for *caigan*?

Your Own Answer_____

Q23

What are the two past subjunctive forms for *gradúes*?

Your Own Answer_____

Q24

What are the two past subjunctive forms for *vayamos*?

Your Own Answer_____

Correct Answers

A22

cayeran/cayesen

A23

graduaras/graduases

A24

fuéramos/fuésemos

Questions

Q25

What are the two past subjunctive forms for *valgan*?

*Your Own Answer*_____

Q26

What are the two past subjunctive forms for *alcen*?

*Your Own Answer*_____

Q27

What are the two past subjunctive forms for *nos riamos*?

*Your Own Answer*_____

Correct Answers

A25

valieran/valiesen

A26

alzara/alzase

A27

nos riéramos/nos riésemos

Questions

Q28

What are the two past subjunctive forms for *muera*?

Your Own Answer_____

Q29

What are the two past subjunctive forms for *conduzcas*?

Your Own Answer_____

Q30

What are the two past subjunctive forms for *durmamos*?

Your Own Answer_____

Correct Answers

A28

muriera/muriese

A29

condujeras/condujeses

A30

durmiéramos/durmiésemos

Questions

Q31

What are the two past subjunctive forms for *estén*?

Your Own Answer_____

Q32

What are the two past subjunctive forms for *pidáis*?

Your Own Answer_____

Q33

What are the two past subjunctive forms for *jueguen*?

Your Own Answer_____

Correct Answers

A31

estuvieran/estuviesen

A32

pidierais/pidieseis

A33

jugaran/jugasen

Questions

Q34

What are the two past subjunctive forms for *tengas*?

Your Own Answer_____

Q35

What are the two past subjunctive forms for *se siente*?

Your Own Answer_____

Q36

What are the two past subjunctive forms for *nos sintamos*?

Your Own Answer_____

Correct Answers

A34

tuvieras/tuvieses

A35

se sentara/se sentase

A36

nos sintiéramos/nos sintiésemos

Questions

Q37

What are the two past subjunctive forms for *oigan*?

Your Own Answer_____

Q38

What are the two past subjunctive forms for *deis*?

Your Own Answer_____

Q39

What are the two past subjunctive forms for *huyamos*?

Your Own Answer_____

Correct Answers

A37

oyeran/oyesen

A38

dierais/dieseis

A39

huyéramos/huyésemos

Questions

Q40

What are the two past subjunctive forms for *empiece*?

Your Own Answer_____

Q41

What are the two past subjunctive forms for *hagas*?

Your Own Answer_____

Q42

What are the two past subjunctive forms for *distingan*?

Your Own Answer_____

Correct Answers

A40

empezara/empezase

A41

hicieras/hicieses

A42

distinguieran/distinguiesen

Questions

Q43

María quería que Juan (IR).

Your Own Answer_____

Q44

Si (TENER) el tiempo, estudiaría más.

Your Own Answer_____

Q45

Pídale a Paco que (HACER) la tarea.

Your Own Answer_____

Correct Answers

A43

FUERA/FUESE

A44

TUVIERA/TUVIESE

A45

HAGA

Questions

Q46

Es evidente que (LLOVER) mañana.

Your Own Answer_____

Q47

Quiero hallar una casa que (TENER) tres alcobas.

Your Own Answer_____

Q48

Quienquiera que (SER), no vayas con él.

Your Own Answer_____

Correct Answers

A46

LLOVERÁ/VA A LLOVER

A47

TENGA

A48

SEA

Questions

Q49

Temíamos que los soldados (MORIR).

Your Own Answer_____

Q50

Es obvio que con práctica ellos (GANAR).

Your Own Answer_____

Q51

No había nadie que (SABER) su nombre.

Your Own Answer_____

Correct Answers

A49

MURIERAN/MURIESEN

A50

GANARÁN/VAN A GANAR

A51

SUPIERA/SUPIESE

Questions

Q52

Conozco a un hombre que (HABLAR) tres idiomas.

Your Own Answer_____

Q53

Lo haré antes de que (THEY ARRIVE).

Your Own Answer_____

Q54

Por enferma que (SHE IS), asistirá al concierto.

Your Own Answer_____

Correct Answers

A52

HABLA

A53

LLEGUEN

A54

ESTE

Questions

Q55

(WE SHOULD) comprarlos.

Habla como si la (HE KNEW) bien.

Yo habría sacado una buena nota si (I HAD DONE) la tarea.

*Your Own Answer*_____

Q56

En caso de que (IT IS SUNNY), debes tomar el traje de baño.

*Your Own Answer*_____

Q57

Tengo tres hermanos que (ARE) mayores que yo.

*Your Own Answer*_____

Correct Answers

A55

DEBEMOS
CONOCIERA/CONOCIESE
HUBIERA HECHO/HUBIESE HECHO

A56

HAGA SOL

A57

SON

Questions

Q58

(LET'S GO) al parque este fin de semana.

*Your Own Answer*_____

Q59

(LET'S NOT BE) tarde hoy.

*Your Own Answer*_____

Q60

(LET HER BEGIN) primero esta vez.

*Your Own Answer*_____

Correct Answers

A58

VÁMONOS

A59

NO LLEGUEMOS

A60

QUE ELLA COMIENCE

Questions

Q61

Give the corresponding "familiar" command for *váyase* (go away).

*Your Own Answer*_____

Q62

Give the corresponding "familiar" command for no *se vaya* (don't go away).

*Your Own Answer*_____

Q63

Give the corresponding "familiar" command for *váyanse* (go away).

*Your Own Answer*_____

Correct Answers

A61

vete

A62

no te vayas

A63

iros

Questions

Q64

Give the corresponding "familiar" command for no *se vayan* (don't go away).

Your Own Answer_____

Q65

Give the corresponding "familiar" command for *haga* (do/make).

Your Own Answer_____

Q66

Give the corresponding "familiar" command for *no haga* (don't do/make).

Your Own Answer_____

Correct Answers

A64

no os vayáis

A65

haz

A66

no hagas

Questions

Q67

Give the corresponding "familiar" command for *hagan* (do/make).

Your Own Answer_____

Q68

Give the corresponding "familiar" command for *no hagan* (don't do/make).

Your Own Answer_____

Q69

Give the corresponding "familiar" command for *sea* (be).

Your Own Answer_____

Correct Answers

A67

haced

A68

no hagáis

A69

sé

Questions

Q70

Give the corresponding "familiar" command for *sean* (be).

*Your Own Answer*_____

Q71

Give the corresponding "familiar" command for *no sea* (don't be).

*Your Own Answer*_____

Q72

Give the corresponding "familiar" command for *no sean* (don't be).

*Your Own Answer*_____

Correct Answers

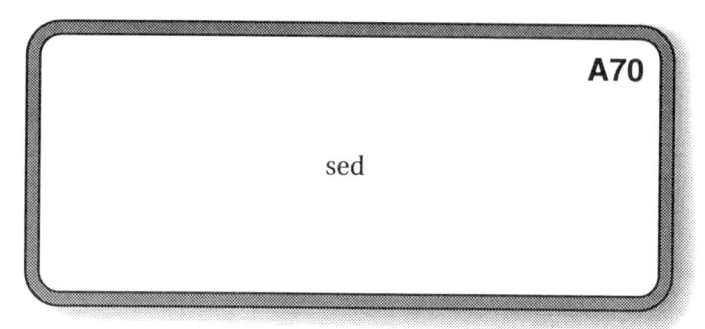

A70

sed

A71

no seas

A72

no seáis

Questions

Q73

Give the corresponding "familiar" command for *traiga* (bring).

*Your Own Answer*_____

Q74

Give the corresponding "familiar" command for *traigan* (bring).

*Your Own Answer*_____

Q75

Give the corresponding "familiar" command for *no traiga* (don't bring).

*Your Own Answer*_____

Correct Answers

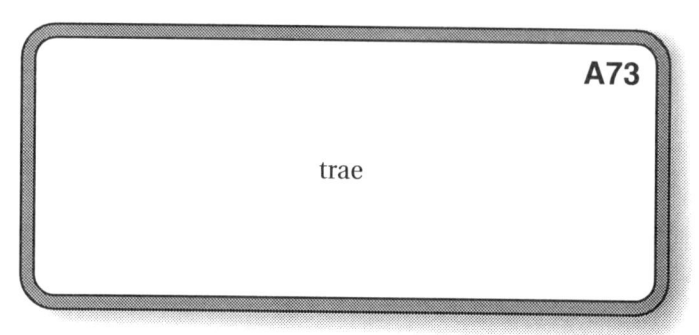

A73

trae

A74

traed

A75

no traigas

Questions

Q76

Give the corresponding "familiar" command for *no traigan* (don't bring).

*Your Own Answer*_____

Q77

Give the corresponding "familiar" command for *duérmase* (go to sleep).

*Your Own Answer*_____

Q78

Give the corresponding "familiar" command for *duérmanse* (go to sleep).

*Your Own Answer*_____

Correct Answers

A76

no traigáis

A77

duérmete

A78

dormíos

Questions

Q79

Give the corresponding "familiar" command for *no se duerma* (don't go to sleep).

*Your Own Answer*_____

Q80

Give the corresponding "familiar" command for *no se duerman* (don't go to sleep).

*Your Own Answer*_____

Q81

Give the corresponding "familiar" command for *escoja* (choose).

*Your Own Answer*_____

Correct Answers

A79

no te duermas

A80

no os durmáis

A81

escoge

Questions

Q82

Give the corresponding "familiar" command for *escojan* (choose).

*Your Own Answer*_____

Q83

Give the corresponding "familiar" command for *no escoja* (don't choose).

*Your Own Answer*_____

Q84

Give the corresponding "familiar" command for *no escojan* (don't choose).

*Your Own Answer*_____

Correct Answers

A82

escoged

A83

no escojas

A84

no escojáis

Questions

Q85

Give the corresponding "familiar" command for *sigan* (follow/continue).

*Your Own Answer*_____

Q86

Give the corresponding "familiar" command for *siga* (follow/continue).

*Your Own Answer*_____

Q87

Give the corresponding "familiar" command for *no sigan* (don't follow/continue).

*Your Own Answer*_____

Correct Answers

A85

seguid

A86

sigue

A87

no sigáis

Questions

Q88

Give the corresponding "familiar" command for *no siga* (don't follow/continue).

Your Own Answer_____

Q89

Give the corresponding "familiar" command for *siéntense* (sit down).

Your Own Answer_____

Q90

Give the corresponding "familiar" command for *siéntese* (sit down).

Your Own Answer_____

Correct Answers

A88

no sigas

A89

sentaos

A90

siéntate

Questions

Q91

Give the corresponding "familiar" command for *no se siente* (don't sit down).

Your Own Answer_____

Q92

Give the corresponding "familiar" command for *no se sienten* (don't sit down).

Your Own Answer_____

Q93

Give the corresponding "familiar" command for *ponga* (put).

Your Own Answer_____

Correct Answers

A91

no te sientes

A92

no os sentéis

A93

pon

Questions

Q94

Give the corresponding "familiar" command for *no ponga* (don't put).

Your Own Answer_____

Q95

Give the corresponding "familiar" command for *pongan* (put).

Your Own Answer_____

Q96

Give the corresponding "familiar" command for *no pongan* (don't put).

Your Own Answer_____

Correct Answers

A94

no pongas

A95

poned

A96

no pongáis

Questions

Q97

Give the corresponding "familiar" command for *póngase* (put on/become)

*Your Own Answer*_____

Q98

Give the corresponding "familiar" command for *no se ponga* (don't put on).

*Your Own Answer*_____

Q99

Give the corresponding "familiar" command for *pónganse* (put on/become).

*Your Own Answer*_____

Correct Answers

A97

ponte

A98

no te pongas

A99

poneos

Questions

Q100

Give the corresponding "familiar" command for *no se pongan* (don't put on).

*Your Own Answer*_____

Q101

Give the corresponding "familiar" command for *ríase* (laugh).

*Your Own Answer*_____

Q102

Give the corresponding "familiar" command for *ríanse* (laugh).

*Your Own Answer*_____

Correct Answers

A100

no os pongáis

A101

ríete

A102

reíos

Questions

Q103

Give the corresponding "familiar" command for *no se ría* (don't laugh).

*Your Own Answer*_____

Q104

Give the corresponding "familiar" command for *no se rían* (don't laugh).

*Your Own Answer*_____

Q105

Give the corresponding "familiar" command for *muérase* (die).

*Your Own Answer*_____

Correct Answers

A103

no te rías

A104

no os riáis

A105

muérete

Questions

Q106

Give the corresponding "familiar" command for *muéranse* (die).

*Your Own Answer*_____

Q107

Give the corresponding "familiar" command for *no se muera* (don't die).

*Your Own Answer*_____

Q108

Give the corresponding "familiar" command for *no se mueran* (don't die).

*Your Own Answer*_____

Correct Answers

A106

moríos

A107

no te mueras

A108

no os muráis

Questions

Q109

Give the corresponding "familiar" command for *diga* (say).

*Your Own Answer*_____

Q110

Give the corresponding "familiar" command for *digan* (say).

*Your Own Answer*_____

Q111

Give the corresponding "familiar" command for *no diga* (don't say).

*Your Own Answer*_____

Correct Answers

A109

di

A110

decid

A111

no digas

Questions

Q112

Give the corresponding "familiar" command for *no digan* (don't say).

Your Own Answer_____

Q113

Give the corresponding "familiar" command for *gradúese* (graduate).

Your Own Answer_____

Q114

Give the corresponding "familiar" command for *gradúense* (graduate).

Your Own Answer_____

Correct Answers

A112

no digáis

A113

gradúate

A114

graduaos

Questions

Q115

Give the corresponding "familiar" command for *no se gradúe* (don't graduate).

Your Own Answer_____

Q116

Give the corresponding "familiar" command for *no se gradúen* (don't graduate).

Your Own Answer_____

Q117

Give the corresponding "familiar" command for *venza* (conquer).

Your Own Answer_____

Correct Answers

A115

no te gradues

A116

no os graduéis

A117

vence

Questions

Q118

Give the corresponding "familiar" command for *venzan* (conquer).

Your Own Answer_____

Q119

Give the corresponding "familiar" command for *no venzan* (don't conquer).

Your Own Answer_____

Q120

Give the corresponding "familiar" command for *no venza* (don't conquer).

Your Own Answer_____

Correct Answers

A118

venced

A119

no venzáis

A120

no venzas

Questions

Q121

Give the corresponding "familiar" command for *empiece* (begin).

Your Own Answer_____

Q122

Give the corresponding "familiar" command for *empiecen* (begin).

Your Own Answer_____

Q123

Give the corresponding "familiar" command for *no empiece* (don't begin).

Your Own Answer_____

Correct Answers

A121

empieza

A122

empezad

A123

no empieces

Questions

Q124

Give the corresponding "familiar" command for *no empiecen* (don't begin).

*Your Own Answer*_____

Q125

Give the corresponding "familiar" command for *riegue* (water).

*Your Own Answer*_____

Q126

Give the corresponding "familiar" command for *rieguen* (water).

*Your Own Answer*_____

Correct Answers

A124

no empecéis

A125

riega

A126

regad

Questions

Q127

Give the corresponding "familiar" command for *no riegue* (don't water).

Your Own Answer_____

Q128

Give the corresponding "familiar" command for *no rieguen* (don't water).

Your Own Answer_____

Q129

Give the corresponding "familiar" command for *huyan* (flee).

Your Own Answer_____

Correct Answers

A127

no riegues

A128

no reguéis

A129

huid

Questions

Q130

Give the corresponding "familiar" command for *huya* (flee).

Your Own Answer_____

Q131

Give the corresponding "familiar" command for *no huya* (don't flee).

Your Own Answer_____

Q132

Give the corresponding "familiar" command for *no huyan* (don't flee).

Your Own Answer_____

Correct Answers

A130

huye

A131

no huyas

A132

no huyáis

Questions

Q133

Give the corresponding "formal" command for *vete* (go away).

Your Own Answer_____

Q134

Give the corresponding "formal" command for *no te vayas* (don't go away).

Your Own Answer_____

Q135

Give the corresponding "formal" command for *idos* (go away).

Your Own Answer_____

Correct Answers

A133

váyase

A134

no se vaya

A135

váyanse

Questions

Q136

Give the corresponding "formal" command for *no os vayáis* (don't go away).

*Your Own Answer*_____

Q137

Give the corresponding "formal" command for *haz* (do/make).

*Your Own Answer*_____

Q138

Give the corresponding "formal" command for *no hagas* (don't do/make).

*Your Own Answer*_____

Correct Answers

A136

no se vayan

A137

haga

A138

no haga

Questions

Q139

Give the corresponding "formal" command for *haced* (do/make).

*Your Own Answer*_____

Q140

Give the corresponding "formal" command for no *hagáis* (don't do/make).

*Your Own Answer*_____

Q141

Give the corresponding "formal" command for *sé* (be).

*Your Own Answer*_____

Correct Answers

A139

hagan

A140

no hagan

A141

sea

Questions

Q142

Give the corresponding "formal" command for *sed* (be).

*Your Own Answer*_____

Q143

Give the corresponding "formal" command for *no seas* (don't be).

*Your Own Answer*_____

Q144

Give the corresponding "formal" command for *no seáis* (don't be).

*Your Own Answer*_____

Correct Answers

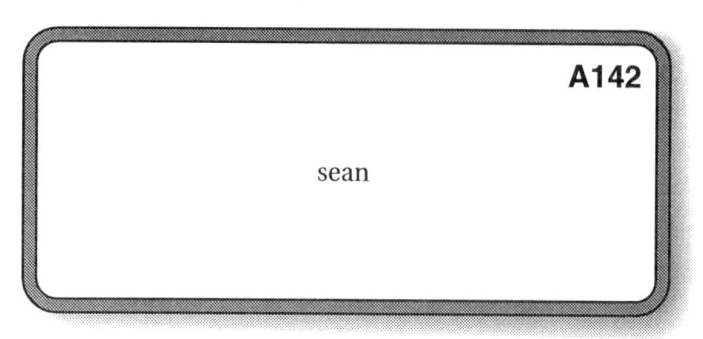

A142

sean

A143

no sea

A144

no sean

Questions

Q145

Give the corresponding "formal" command for *trae* (bring).

*Your Own Answer*_____

Q146

Give the corresponding "formal" command for *traed* (bring).

*Your Own Answer*_____

Q147

Give the corresponding "formal" command for *no traigas* (don't bring).

*Your Own Answer*_____

Correct Answers

A145

traiga

A146

traigan

A147

no traiga

Questions

Q148

Give the corresponding "formal" command for *no traigáis* (don't bring).

*Your Own Answer*_____

Q149

Give the corresponding "formal" command for *duérmete* (go to sleep).

*Your Own Answer*_____

Q150

Give the corresponding "formal" command for *dormíos* (go to sleep).

*Your Own Answer*_____

Correct Answers

A148

no traigan

A149

duérmase

A150

duérmanse

Questions

Q151

Give the corresponding "formal" command for *no os durmáis* (don't go to sleep).

Your Own Answer_____

Q152

Give the corresponding "formal" command for *no te duermas* (don't go to sleep).

Your Own Answer_____

Q153

Give the corresponding "formal" command for *escoge* (choose).

Your Own Answer_____

Correct Answers

A151

no se duerman

A152

no se duerma

A153

escoja

Questions

Q154

Give the corresponding "formal" command for *no escojas* (don't choose).

*Your Own Answer*_____

Q155

Give the corresponding "formal" command for *escoged* (choose).

*Your Own Answer*_____

Q156

Give the corresponding "formal" command for *no escojáis* (don't choose).

*Your Own Answer*_____

Correct Answers

A154

no escoja

A155

escojan

A156

no escojan

Questions

Q157

Give the corresponding "formal" command for *seguid* (follow/continue).

Your Own Answer_____

Q158

Give the corresponding "formal" command for *sigue* (follow/continue).

Your Own Answer_____

Q159

Give the corresponding "formal" command for *no sigáis* (don't follow/continue).

Your Own Answer_____

Correct Answers

A157

sigan

A158

siga

A159

no sigan

Questions

Q160

Give the corresponding "formal" command for *no sigas* (don't follow/continue).

*Your Own Answer*_____

Q161

Give the corresponding "formal" command for *sentaos* (sit down).

*Your Own Answer*_____

Q162

Give the corresponding "formal" command for *siéntate* (sit down).

*Your Own Answer*_____

Correct Answers

A160

no siga

A161

siéntense

A162

siéntese

Questions

Q163

Give the corresponding "formal" command for *no te sientes* (don't sit down).

Your Own Answer_____

Q164

Give the corresponding "formal" command for *no os sentéis* (don't sit down).

Your Own Answer_____

Q165

Give the corresponding "formal" command for *pon* (put).

Your Own Answer_____

Correct Answers

A163

no se siente

A164

no se sienten

A165

ponga

Questions

Q166

Give the corresponding "formal" command for *no pongas* (don't put).

Your Own Answer_____

Q167

Give the corresponding "formal" command for *poned* (put).

Your Own Answer_____

Q168

Give the corresponding "formal" command for *no pongáis* (don't put).

Your Own Answer_____

Correct Answers

A166

no ponga

A167

pongan

A168

no pongan

Questions

Q169

Give the corresponding "formal" command for *ponte* (put on/become).

Your Own Answer___

Q170

Give the corresponding "formal" command for *no te pongas* (don't put on).

Your Own Answer___

Q171

Give the corresponding "formal" command for *poneos* (put on/become).

Your Own Answer___

Correct Answers

A169

póngase

A170

no se ponga

A171

pónganse

Questions

Q172

Give the corresponding "formal" command for *no os pongáis* (don't put on).

Your Own Answer_____

Q173

Give the corresponding "formal" command for *ríete* (laugh).

Your Own Answer_____

Q174

Give the corresponding "formal" command for *reíos* (laugh).

Your Own Answer_____

Correct Answers

A172

no se pongan

A173

ríase

A174

ríanse

Questions

Q175

Give the corresponding "formal" command for *no te rías* (don't laugh).

Your Own Answer_____

Q176

Give the corresponding "formal" command for *no os riáis* (don't laugh).

Your Own Answer_____

Q177

Give the corresponding "formal" command for *muérete* (die).

Your Own Answer_____

Correct Answers

A175

no se ría

A176

no se rían

A177

muérase

Questions

Q178

Give the corresponding "formal" command for *moríos* (die).

*Your Own Answer*_____

Q179

Give the corresponding "formal" command for *no os muráis* (don't die).

*Your Own Answer*_____

Q180

Give the corresponding "formal" command for *no te mueras* (don't die).

*Your Own Answer*_____

Correct Answers

A178

muéranse

A179

no se mueran

A180

no se muera

Questions

Q181

Give the corresponding "formal" command for *di* (say).

Your Own Answer_____

Q182

Give the corresponding "formal" command for *decid* (say).

Your Own Answer_____

Q183

Give the corresponding "formal" command for *no digas* (don't say).

Your Own Answer_____

Correct Answers

A181

diga

A182

digan

A183

no diga

Questions

Q184

Give the corresponding "formal" command for *no digáis* (don't say).

*Your Own Answer*_____

Q185

Give the corresponding "formal" command for *gradúate* (graduate).

*Your Own Answer*_____

Q186

Give the corresponding "formal" command for *graduaos* (graduate).

*Your Own Answer*_____

Correct Answers

A184

no digan

A185

gradúese

A186

gradúense

Questions

Q187

Give the corresponding "formal" command for *no te gradues* (don't graduate).

*Your Own Answer*_____

Q188

Give the corresponding "formal" command for *no os graduéis* (don't graduate).

*Your Own Answer*_____

Q189

Give the corresponding "formal" command for *vence* (conquer).

*Your Own Answer*_____

Correct Answers

A187

no se gradúe

A188

no se gradúen

A189

venza

Questions

Q190

Give the corresponding "formal" command for *venced* (conquer).

*Your Own Answer*_____

Q191

Give the corresponding "formal" command for *no venzáis* (don't conquer).

*Your Own Answer*_____

Q192

Give the corresponding "formal" command for *no venzas* (don't conquer).

*Your Own Answer*_____

Correct Answers

A190

venzan

A191

no venzan

A192

no venza

Questions

Q193

Give the corresponding "formal" command for *empieza* (begin).

Your Own Answer_____

Q194

Give the corresponding "formal" command for *empezad* (begin).

Your Own Answer_____

Q195

Give the corresponding "formal" command for *no empieces* (don't begin).

Your Own Answer_____

Correct Answers

A193

empiece

A194

empiecen

A195

no empiece

Questions

Q196

Give the corresponding "formal" command for *no empecéis* (don't begin).

Your Own Answer_____

Q197

Give the corresponding "formal" command for *riega* (water).

Your Own Answer_____

Q198

Give the corresponding "formal" command for *regad* (water).

Your Own Answer_____

Correct Answers

A196

no empiecen

A197

riegue

A198

rieguen

Questions

Q199

Give the corresponding "formal" command for *no riegues* (don't water).

Your Own Answer_____

Q200

Give the corresponding "formal" command for *no requéis* (don't water).

Your Own Answer_____

Q201

Give the corresponding "formal" command for *huid* (flee).

Your Own Answer_____

Correct Answers

A199

no riegue

A200

no rieguen

A201

huyan

Questions

Q202

Give the corresponding "formal" command for *huye* (flee).

Your Own Answer_____

Q203

Give the corresponding "formal" command for *no huyas* (don't flee).

Your Own Answer_____

Q204

Give the corresponding "formal" command for *no huyáis* (don't flee).

Your Own Answer_____

Correct Answers

A202

huya

A203

no huya

A204

no huyan

Questions

Q205

Hijos, ¡(GO TO BED or LIE DOWN) ahora!

*Your Own Answer*_____

Q206

Paco, ¡(DON'T BE) un estudiante malo!

*Your Own Answer*_____

Q207

Antes de levantarte, ¡(STUDY) los verbos!

*Your Own Answer*_____

Correct Answers

A205

ACUÉSTENSE or ACOSTAOS

A206

NO SEAS

A207

ESTUDIA

Questions

Q208

Señor, ¡(DON'T PUNISH) a su hijo tanto!

*Your Own Answer*_____

Q209

Amigos, ¡(BRING) los discos a mi casa!

*Your Own Answer*_____

Q210

Hija mía, ¡(DON'T TOUCH) esa pintura!

*Your Own Answer*_____

Correct Answers

A208

NO CASTIGUE

A209

TRAED or TRAIGAN

A210

NO TOQUES

Questions

Q211

Señores, ¡(DON'T PAY) hasta el fin!

Your Own Answer_____

Q212

Niños, ¡(EAT UP) los vegetales ahora!

Your Own Answer_____

Q213

Hijo mío, ¡(DON'T SLIDE) sobre el hielo!

Your Own Answer_____

Correct Answers

A211

NO PAGUEN

A212

CÓMANSE or COMEOS

A213

NO DESLICES

Questions

Q214

(TELL ME) la verdad, le dijo la mujer a su novio.

Your Own Answer_____

Q215

Señor Gómez, ¡(GET UP) ahora mismo!

Your Own Answer_____

Q216

No te (GO TO BED) en el cuarto de Felipe.

Your Own Answer_____

Correct Answers

A214

DIME

A215

LEVÁNTESE

A216

ACUESTES

Questions

Q217

Hola, ¡(SIT DOWN) para hablar conmigo!

Your Own Answer_____

Q218

Antes de salir mi mamá me dijo. ¡(PUT ON) el abrigo, hijo!

Your Own Answer_____

Q219

Hijos, no (LAUGH) mientras estoy hablando.

Your Own Answer_____

Correct Answers

A217

SENTAOS or SIÉNTENSE

A218

PONTE

A219

OS RIÁIS or SE RÍAN

Questions

Q220

(LET'S SIT DOWN) aquí para poder ver mejor.

Your Own Answer_____

Q221

What is the corresponding preterite form for *dirijo* (I direct)?

Your Own Answer_____

Q222

What is the corresponding preterite form for *produces* (you produce)?

Your Own Answer_____

Correct Answers

A220

SENTÉMONOS

A221

dirigí

A222

produjiste

Questions

Q223

What is the corresponding preterite form for *dice* (he says)?

Your Own Answer_____

Q224

What is the corresponding preterite form for *traemos* (we bring)?

Your Own Answer_____

Q225

What is the corresponding preterite form for *huyen* (they flee)?

Your Own Answer_____

Correct Answers

A223

dijo

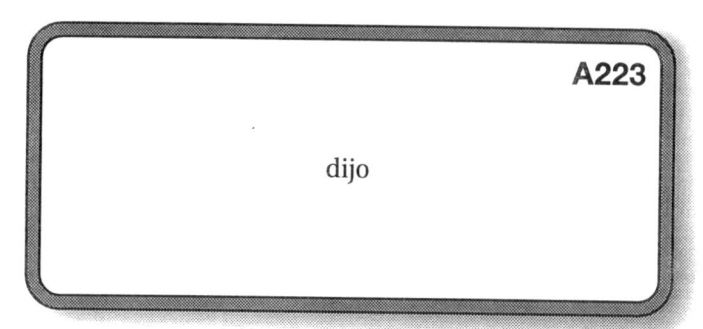

A224

trajimos

A225

huyeron

Questions

Q226

What is the corresponding preterite form for *pido* (I ask for)?

*Your Own Answer*_____

Q227

What is the corresponding preterite form for *vais* (you go)?

*Your Own Answer*_____

Q228

What is the corresponding preterite form for *eres* (you are)

*Your Own Answer*_____

Correct Answers

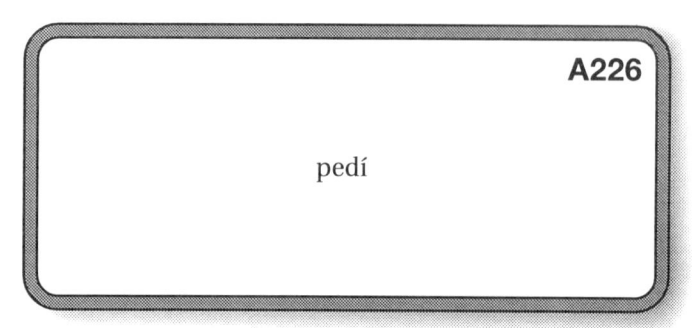

A226

pedí

A227

fuisteis

A228

fuiste

Questions

Q229

What is the corresponding preterite form for *almuerzo* (I eat lunch)?

*Your Own Answer*_____

Q230

What is the corresponding preterite form for *sigue* (he follows)?

*Your Own Answer*_____

Q231

What is the corresponding preterite form for *mueren* (they die)?

*Your Own Answer*_____

Correct Answers

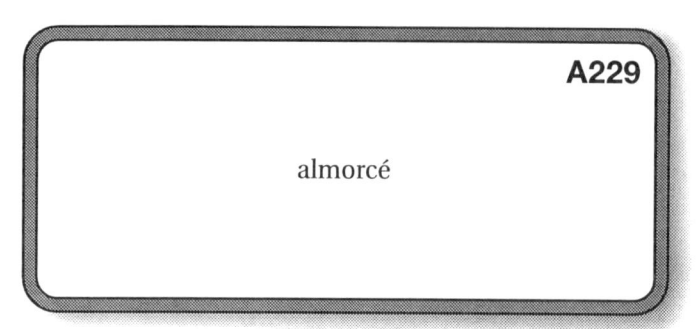

A229

almorcé

A230

siguió

A231

murieron

Questions

Q232

What is the corresponding preterite form for *se divierte* (he enjoys)?

*Your Own Answer*_____

Q233

What is the corresponding preterite form for *quepo* (I fit)?

*Your Own Answer*_____

Q234

What is the corresponding preterite form for *ves* (you see)?

*Your Own Answer*_____

Correct Answers

A232

se divirtió

A233

cupe

A234

viste

Questions

Q235

What is the corresponding preterite form for *sé* (I know)?

Your Own Answer_____

Q236

What is the corresponding preterite form for *están* (they are)?

Your Own Answer_____

Q237

What is the corresponding preterite form for *vienen* (they come)?

Your Own Answer_____

Correct Answers

A235

supe

A236

estuvieron

A237

vinieron

Questions

Q238

What is the corresponding preterite form for *tengo* (I have)?

*Your Own Answer*_____

Q239

What is the corresponding preterite form for *haces* (you make/do)?

*Your Own Answer*_____

Q240

What is the corresponding preterite form for *te sientes* (you feel)?

*Your Own Answer*_____

Correct Answers

A238

tuve

A239

hiciste

A240

te sentiste

Questions

Q241

What is the corresponding preterite form for *te sientas* (you sit down)?

Your Own Answer_____

Q242

What is the corresponding preterite form for *se caen* (they fall down)?

Your Own Answer_____

Q243

What is the corresponding preterite form for *lees* (you read)?

Your Own Answer_____

Correct Answers

A241

te sentaste

A242

se cayeron

A243

leíste

Questions

Q244

What is the corresponding preterite form for *me río* (I laugh)?

*Your Own Answer*_____

Q245

What is the corresponding preterite form for *elijo* (I elect)?

*Your Own Answer*_____

Q246

What is the corresponding preterite form for *actúas* (you act)?

*Your Own Answer*_____

Correct Answers

A244

me reí

A245

elegí

A246

actuaste

Questions

Q247

What is the corresponding preterite form for *huele* (it smells)?

Your Own Answer_____

Q248

What is the corresponding preterite form for *empiezo* (I begin)?

Your Own Answer_____

Q249

What is the corresponding imperfect form for *dirijo* (I direct)?

Your Own Answer_____

Correct Answers

A247

olió

A248

empecé

A249

dirigía

Questions

Q250

What is the corresponding imperfect form for *produces* (you produce)?

*Your Own Answer*_____

Q251

What is the corresponding imperfect form for *dice* (he says)?

*Your Own Answer*_____

Q252

What is the corresponding imperfect form *traemos* (we bring)?

*Your Own Answer*_____

Correct Answers

A250

producías

A251

decía

A252

traíamos

Questions

Q253

What is the corresponding imperfect form for *huyen* (they flee)?

*Your Own Answer*_____

Q254

What is the corresponding imperfect form for *pido* (I ask for)?

*Your Own Answer*_____

Q255

What is the corresponding imperfect form for *vais* (you go)?

*Your Own Answer*_____

Correct Answers

A253

huían

A254

pedía

A255

ibais

Questions

Q256

What is the corresponding imperfect form for *eres* (you are)?

Your Own Answer_____

Q257

What is the corresponding imperfect form for *almuerzo* (I eat lunch)?

Your Own Answer_____

Q258

What is the corresponding imperfect form for *sigue* (he follows)?

Your Own Answer_____

Correct Answers

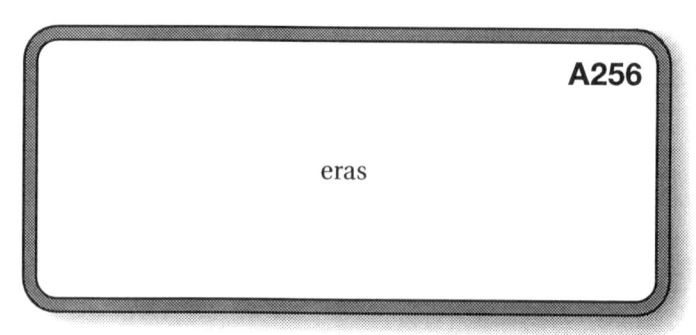

A256

eras

A257

almorzaba

A258

seguía

Questions

Q259

What is the corresponding imperfect form for *mueren* (they die)?

Your Own Answer_____

Q260

What is the corresponding imperfect form for *se divierte* (he enjoys)?

Your Own Answer_____

Q261

What is the corresponding imperfect form for *quepo* (I fit)?

Your Own Answer_____

Correct Answers

A259

morían

A260

se divertía

A261

cabía

Questions

Q262

What is the corresponding imperfect form for *ves* (you see)?

Your Own Answer_____

Q263

What is the corresponding imperfect form for *sé* (I know)?

Your Own Answer_____

Q264

What is the corresponding imperfect form for *están* (they are)?

Your Own Answer_____

Correct Answers

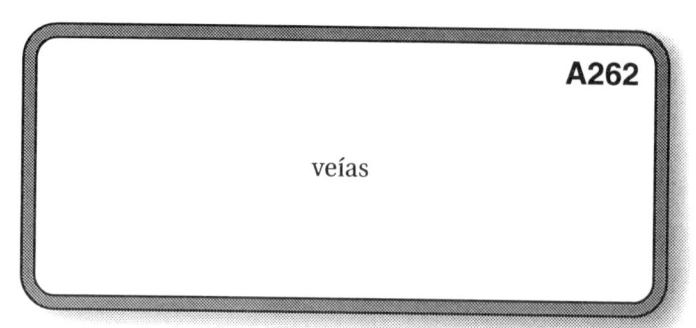

A262

veías

A263

sabía

A264

estaban

Questions

Q265

What is the corresponding imperfect form for *vienen* (they come)?

Your Own Answer_____

Q266

What is the corresponding imperfect form for *tengo* (I have)?

Your Own Answer_____

Q267

What is the corresponding imperfect form for *haces* (you make/do)?

Your Own Answer_____

Correct Answers

A265

venían

A266

tenía

A267

hacías

Questions

Q268

What is the corresponding imperfect form for *te sientes* (you feel)?

Your Own Answer_____

Q269

What is the corresponding imperfect form for *te sientas* (you sit down)?

Your Own Answer_____

Q270

What is the corresponding imperfect form for *se caen* (they fall down)?

Your Own Answer_____

Correct Answers

A268

te sentías

A269

te sentabas

A270

se caían

Questions

Q271

What is the corresponding imperfect form for *lees* (you read)?

Your Own Answer_____

Q272

What is the corresponding imperfect form for *me río* (I laugh)?

Your Own Answer_____

Q273

What is the corresponding imperfect form for *elijo* (I elect)?

Your Own Answer_____

Correct Answers

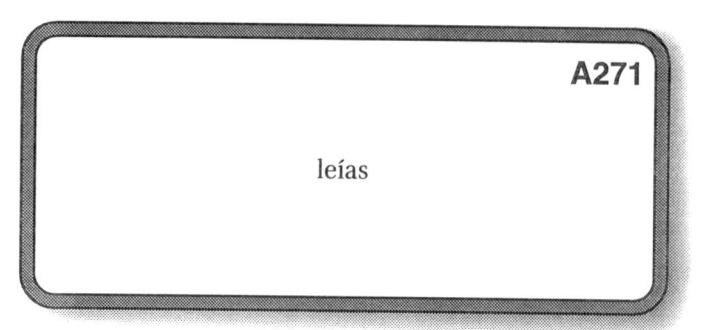

A271

leías

A272

me reía

A273

elegía

Questions

Q274

What is the corresponding imperfect form for *actúas* (you act)?

Your Own Answer_____

Q275

What is the corresponding imperfect form for *huele* (it smells)?

Your Own Answer_____

Q276

What is the corresponding imperfect form for *empiezo* (I begin)?

Your Own Answer_____

Correct Answers

A274

actuabas

A275

olía

A276

empezaba

Questions

Q277

What does *conocer* in the preterite mean?

Your Own Answer_____

Q278

What does *saber* in the preterite mean?

Your Own Answer_____

Q279

What does *poder* in the preterite mean?

Your Own Answer_____

Correct Answers

A277

met

A278

found out

A279

managed

Questions

Q280

(IT WAS) las diez cuando salieron.

*Your Own Answer*_____

Q281

De pronto Juan (DARSE CUENTA) de su error.

*Your Own Answer*_____

Q282

¿Cuánto tiempo hacía que María (APRENDER) el español?

*Your Own Answer*_____

Correct Answers

A280

ERAN

A281

SE DIÓ CUENTA

A282

APRENDÍA

Questions

Q283

Cuando (I WAS) joven, tenía un gato.

*Your Own Answer*___

Q284

(THERE WAS) un terremoto ayer en Japón.

*Your Own Answer*___

Q285

El sábado pasado el hombre (MORIR).

*Your Own Answer*___

Correct Answers

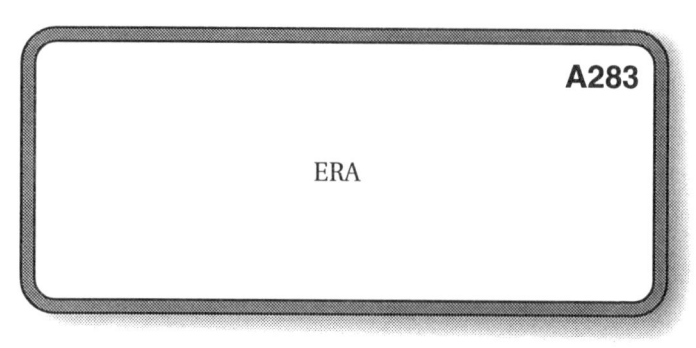

A283

ERA

A284

HUBO

A285

MURIÓ

Questions

Q286

Cada verano (WE WOULD GO) allí.

*Your Own Answer*___

Q287

En ese momento el juez (BELIEVED) al testigo.

*Your Own Answer*___

Q288

(THEY HAD JUST) terminar cuando entré.

*Your Own Answer*___

Correct Answers

A286

ÍBAMOS

A287

CREYÓ

A288

ACABABAN DE

Questions

Q289

Hace dos años que mi amigo (RETURNED) de España.

*Your Own Answer*_____

Q290

Esta mañana al levantarme (SENTIRSE) triste.

*Your Own Answer*_____

Q291

Mientras Juan (HACER) la tarea, escuchaba la radio.

*Your Own Answer*_____

Correct Answers

A289

VOLVIÓ

A290

ME SENTÍ

A291

HACÍA

Questions

Q292

Anoche yo (ESTAR) en el cine hasta las doce.

*Your Own Answer*_____

Q293

Hace tres meses que mi amigo (STUDIED) allí.

*Your Own Answer*_____

Q294

(THEY WERE READING) cuando el teléfono sonó.

*Your Own Answer*_____

Correct Answers

A292

ESTUVE

A293

ESTUDIÓ

A294

LEÍAN

Questions

Q295

(I BEGAN) a llorar al ver a mi hijo sufrir.

Your Own Answer_____

Q296

Al entrar (HE THOUGHT) que vió a un fantasma.

Your Own Answer_____

Q297

(THERE WERE) varios cuartos para alquilar.

Your Own Answer_____

Correct Answers

A295

EMPECÉ or COMENCÉ

A296

PENSÓ

A297

HABÍA

Questions

Q298

La guerra de Vietnam (DURAR) muchos años.

Your Own Answer_____

Q299

Entré por la puerta que (ESTAR) cerrada con llave.

Your Own Answer_____

Q300

El cielo (WAS) azul.

Your Own Answer_____

Correct Answers

A298

DURÓ

A299

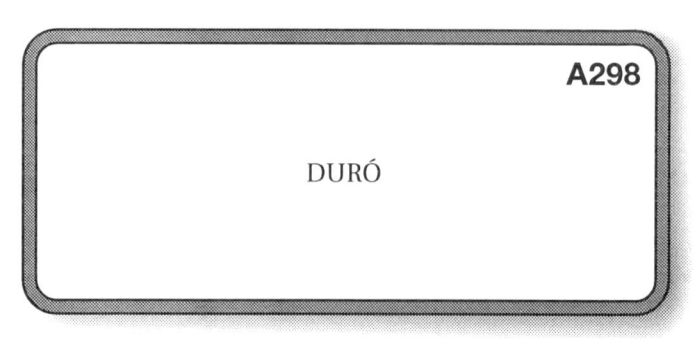

ESTABA

A300

ERA

Questions

Q301

Durante su niñez, Juan (TO GO) al cine a menudo.

*Your Own Answer*_____

Q302

Ayer yo (SABER) su dirección por primera vez.

*Your Own Answer*_____

Q303

¿Cuánto tiempo (HACER) que andabas sin coche?

*Your Own Answer*_____

Correct Answers

A301

IBA

A302

SUPE

A303

HACÍA

Questions

Q304

Aunque mi amigo entró, no lo (VER).

*Your Own Answer*___

Q305

Estaba seguro que (IT WAS RAINING).

*Your Own Answer*___

Q306

El profesor siempre (CONSULTAR) el diccionario.

*Your Own Answer*___

Correct Answers

A304

VÍ

A305

LLOUÍA/ESTABA LLOVIENDO

A306

CONSULTABA

Questions

Q307

El ladrón (LLEVAR) una chaqueta de cuero.

*Your Own Answer*_____

Q308

Cuando éramos ricos, (VIAJAR) mucho.

*Your Own Answer*_____

Q309

Era la una cuando los hijos (VOLVER).

*Your Own Answer*_____

Correct Answers

A307

LLEVABA

A308

VIAJÁBAMOS

A309

VOLVIERON

Questions

Q310

Ayer mientras yo (VESTIRSE), mi hermana (BAÑARSE).

Your Own Answer

Q311

Cuando era joven, ella me (ESCRIBIR).

Your Own Answer

Q312

De súbito ellos (OLER) humo ayer.

Your Own Answer

Correct Answers

A310

ME VESTÍA; SE BAÑABA

A311

ESCRIBÍA

A312

OLIERON

Questions

Q313

Al andar a la escuela ayer, yo (TROPEZAR) con un amigo mío.

Your Own Answer_____

Q314

Cuando el policía (VER) el accidente, empezó a llorar.

Your Own Answer_____

Q315

Tomé el cheque y lo (CAMBIAR).

Your Own Answer_____

Correct Answers

A313

TROPECÉ

A314

VIO

A315

CAMBIÉ

Questions

Q316

Su casa (WAS) cerca de la Plaza Mayor.

*Your Own Answer*_____

Q317

En este instante (APPEARED) en la ventana la figura de una vieja.

*Your Own Answer*_____

Q318

Los novios (ESTAR) sentados en el sofá cuando los vi.

*Your Own Answer*_____

Correct Answers

A316

ESTABA

A317

APARECIÓ

A318

ESTABAN

Questions

Q319

¿Por qué no me dijiste que (SER) las diez?

Your Own Answer_____

Q320

Al terminar la novela el hombre (CERRAR) el libro.

Your Own Answer_____

Q321

(WE WENT OUT) ayer sin abrigo porque hacía calor.

Your Own Answer_____

Correct Answers

A319

ERAN

A320

CERRÓ

A321

SALIMOS

Questions

Q322

Al acercarme a la casa, vi que (ARDER).

*Your Own Answer*_____

Q323

¿Cuánto tiempo (HAD HE BEEN WAITING) cuando el profesor entró?

*Your Own Answer*_____

Q324

De repente los chicos (HEARD) un tiro.

*Your Own Answer*_____

Correct Answers

A322

ARDÍA

A323

LLEVABA ESPERANDO

A324

OYERON

Questions

Q325

Los moros (WERE) en España ocho siglos.

*Your Own Answer*_____

Q326

Al oír el ruido él (BECAME FRIGHTENED).

*Your Own Answer*_____

Q327

(IT WAS) las diez cuando regresaron.

*Your Own Answer*_____

Correct Answers

A325

ESTUVIERON

A326

SE ASUSTÓ

A327

ERAN

Questions

Q328

Cuando yo (WAS) joven, (I USED TO GO) de compras con mi mamá cada semana.

*Your Own Answer*_____

Q329

(THERE WAS) un terremoto ayer.

*Your Own Answer*_____

Q330

(I MET) a mi esposo en Madrid.

*Your Own Answer*_____

Correct Answers

A328

ERA or IBA

A329

HUBO

A330

CONOCÍ

Questions

Q331

(THEY FOUND OUT) la verdad al leer la carta.

*Your Own Answer*_____

Q332

Hacía tres horas que Juan (HAD BEEN WAITING) en la estación.

*Your Own Answer*_____

Q333

(SHE MADE) la cama al levantarse hoy.

*Your Own Answer*_____

Correct Answers

A331

SUPIERON

A332

ESPERABA

A333

HIZO

Questions

Q334

Al despertarse Ramón se dio cuenta de que (IT WAS RAINING).

*Your Own Answer*_____

Q335

Aunque ella vino temprano, no la (VER).

*Your Own Answer*_____

Q336

Esta tarde mientras (I WAS READING) el periódico, sonó el teléfono.

*Your Own Answer*_____

Correct Answers

A334

LLOVÍA

A335

VI

A336

LEÍA

Questions

Q337

¿Cuánto tiempo (HACER) que andabas sin coche?

*Your Own Answer*_____

Q338

(IT WAS) las tres cuando el tren partió.

*Your Own Answer*_____

Q339

(HACER) dos años que terminó la guerra.

*Your Own Answer*_____

Correct Answers

A337

HACÍA

A338

ERAN

A339

HACE

Questions

Q340

Ayer al oír al testigo, el juez lo (BELIEVED).

*Your Own Answer*___

Q341

¿Cuánto tiempo (HACER) que hablabas cuando entraron?

*Your Own Answer*___

Q342

Gustar and verbs like it are always used with _____ pronouns.

*Your Own Answer*___

Correct Answers

A340

CREYÓ

A341

HACÍA

A342

indirect object

Questions

Q343

Gustar and verbs like it are commonly used in the _____ person singular and plural.

Your Own Answer_____

Q344

In English, the subject of a *gustar/gustar* type sentence becomes the _____ in Spanish.

Your Own Answer_____

Q345

A Juan y a mí _____ gusta comer chocolate.

Your Own Answer_____

Correct Answers

A343

third

A344

indirect object

A345

nos

Questions

Q346

¿A quiénes _____ toca?

Your Own Answer_____

Q347

(THE BOYS) les gusta jugar al golf.

Your Own Answer_____

Q348

_____ os encanta el campo.

Your Own Answer_____

Correct Answers

A346

les

A347

A LOS CHICOS

A348

A vosotros

Questions

Q349

¿Cuántos libros (DID HE HAVE LEFT)?

*Your Own Answer*_____

Q350

(IT PLEASES MARY) bailar cada día.

*Your Own Answer*_____

Q351

(I USED TO LIKE) los coches rojos.

*Your Own Answer*_____

Correct Answers

A349

LE QUEDARON

A350

A MARIÁ LE PLACE/AGRADA

A351

ME GUSTABAN

Questions

Q352

(WE NEED) muchos ejemplos más.

Your Own Answer_____

Q353

A Jaime y a mí (GUSTAR) el cine.

Your Own Answer_____

Q354

(IT SEEMS TO ME) que no tiene bastante dinero.

Your Own Answer_____

Correct Answers

A352

NOS HACEN FALTA

A353

NOS GUSTA

A354

ME PARECE

Questions

Q355

¿A quiénes (TOCAR)?

Your Own Answer_____

Q356

(I ENJOY) gastar dinero.

Your Own Answer_____

Q357

¿(WHO WILL LIKE) acompañarme?

Your Own Answer_____

Correct Answers

A355

LES TOCA

A356

ME ENCANTA

A357

A QUIÉN LE GUSTARÁ

Questions

Q358

A José (IMPORTAR) sus notas.

*Your Own Answer*_____

Q359

Al soldado (DOLER) la pierna rota.

*Your Own Answer*_____

Q360

Espero que a la maestra (TO LIKE) mi tarea.

*Your Own Answer*_____

Correct Answers

A358

LE IMPORTAN

A359

LE DUELE

A360

LE GUSTE

Questions

Q361

(THE FAMILY NEEDS) un coche nuevo.

Your Own Answer_____

Q362

(I LIKE) todas clases de libros.

Your Own Answer_____

Q363

(IT PLEASES US) hacer las tareas.

Your Own Answer_____

Correct Answers

A361

A LA FAMILIA LE HACE FALTA

A362

ME GUSTAN

A363

NOS AGRADA

Questions

Q364

(JUAN NEEDS) mejores notas.

Your Own Answer_____

Q365

(THE STUDENTS DIDN'T LIKE) la idea central de la novela.

Your Own Answer_____

Q366

(MY BOYFRIEND AND I WILL LIKE) el drama si podemos comprar entradas.

Your Own Answer_____

Correct Answers

A364

A JUAN LE HACEN FALTA

A365

A LOS ALUMNOS NO LES GUSTÓ

A366

A MI NOVIO Y A MÍ NOS GUSTARÁ

Questions

Q367

A mis amigos (LIKED) mi coche nuevo.

*Your Own Answer*_____

Q368

¿A quiénes _____ tocó el premio?

*Your Own Answer*_____

Q369

A nosotros (HACER FALTA) cien dólares.

*Your Own Answer*_____

Correct Answers

A367

LES GUSTÓ

A368

les

A369

NOS HACEN FALTA

Questions

Q370

A Jaime y a mí (TO LIKE) la película.

*Your Own Answer*_____

Q371

_____ chico le gusta jugar al fútbol.

*Your Own Answer*_____

Q372

A Roberto _____ gusta ir a la playa durante el verano.

*Your Own Answer*_____

Correct Answers

A370

NOS GUSTA

A371

Al

A372

le

Questions

Q373

A Rob y a mí (TO LIKE) el helado.

Your Own Answer_____

Q374

A Juan (DIDN'T MIND) ir al cine.

Your Own Answer_____

Q375

A nosotros _____ encantó la ciudad.

Your Own Answer_____

Correct Answers

A373

NOS GUSTA

A374

NO LE IMPORTABA

A375

nos

Questions

Q376

¿(HOW MANY) clases tienes?

Your Own Answer_____

Q377

¿(HOW MUCH) dinero necesitas?

Your Own Answer_____

Q378

¿(HOW MUCH) inteligencia requiere el puesto?

Your Own Answer_____

Correct Answers

A376

CUÁNTAS

A377

CUÁNTO

A378

CUÁNTA

Questions

Q379

¿(WHO) es el hombre desconocido?

*Your Own Answer*_____

Q380

¿(WHERE) están las calles más usadas?

*Your Own Answer*_____

Q381

¿(WHICH) abrigo quieres llevar puesto?

*Your Own Answer*_____

Correct Answers

A379

QUIÉN

A380

DÓNDE

A381

QUÉ

Questions

Q382

No sé (WHAT) hacer.

*Your Own Answer*_____

Q383

¡(WHAT A) día tan bello!

*Your Own Answer*_____

Q384

¿(WHAT) es el amor?

*Your Own Answer*_____

Correct Answers

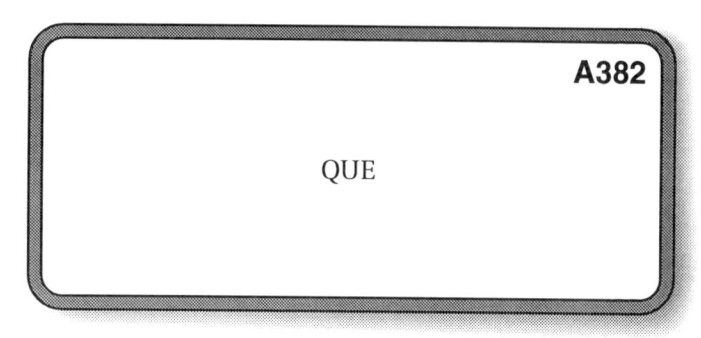

A382

QUE

A383

QUÉ

A384

QUÉ

Questions

Q385

¿(HOW) haces tanto sin ayuda?

*Your Own Answer*_____

Q386

¿(WHY) estudias sin apuntes?

*Your Own Answer*_____

Q387

¿(WHEN) vamos a llegar a Madrid?

*Your Own Answer*_____

Correct Answers

A385

CÓMO

A386

POR QUÉ

A387

CUÁNDO

Questions

Q388

¿(WHAT) es la capital de Francia?

Your Own Answer_____

Q389

La casa (WHERE) vivo es muy vieja.

Your Own Answer_____

Q390

¿(WHOM) ves cada sábado? Veo a María.

Your Own Answer_____

Correct Answers

A388

CUÁL

A389

DONDE

A390

A QUIÉN

Questions

Q391

Mama, ¿(WHAT) sirven los anteojos?

*Your Own Answer*_____

Q392

¿(WHAT) son los días de la semana?

*Your Own Answer*_____

Q393

¿(WHAT) tiempo hace hoy?

*Your Own Answer*_____

Correct Answers

A391

PARA QUÉ

A392

CUÁLES

A393

QUÉ

Questions

Q394

¿(WHO) son los autores más famosos?

*Your Own Answer*_____

Q395

¿(WHERE) vas los sábados?

*Your Own Answer*_____

Q396

¿(HOW MUCH) cuesta el auto?

*Your Own Answer*_____

Correct Answers

A394

QUIÉNES

A395

A DÓNDE

A396

CUÁNTO

Questions

Q397

¿(HOW MANY) días hay en octubre?

*Your Own Answer*_____

Q398

¿(WHICH) abrigo prefieres?

*Your Own Answer*_____

Q399

No sé (WHAT) hacer.

*Your Own Answer*_____

Correct Answers

A397

CUÁNTOS

A398

QUÉ

A399

QUE

Questions

Q400

¡(WHAT A) día tan bello!

*Your Own Answer*_____

Q401

¿(WHICH) de los autores son los más leídos?

*Your Own Answer*_____

Q402

¿(WHOSE) es la casa nueva?

*Your Own Answer*_____

Correct Answers

A400

QUÉ

A401

CUÁLES

A402

DE QUIÉN

Questions

Q403

¿(WHICH) de los hermanos es más alto?

Your Own Answer_____

Q404

No sabe (WHOSE) es el coche nuevo.

Your Own Answer_____

Q405

The common form of "to be" used with the adjective *feliz* is_____.

Your Own Answer_____

Correct Answers

A403

CUÁL

A404

DE QUIÉN

A405

estar

Questions

Q406

To express what one's opinion "is" about something, one uses the verb _____.

Your Own Answer_____

Q407

The helping verb used in the progressive tense is _____.

Your Own Answer_____

Q408

In Spanish, impersonal expressions are a combination of the third singular of _____ and an adjective.

Your Own Answer_____

Correct Answers

A406

ser

A407

estar

A408

ser

Questions

Q409

(IT HAS BEEN) necesario estudiar más.

Your Own Answer_____

Q410

Mis amigos (ARE) hombres contentos.

Your Own Answer_____

Q411

Cuando (I WAS) en España la semana pasada, me divertí mucho.

Your Own Answer_____

Correct Answers

A409

HA SIDO

A410

SON

A411

ESTUVE

Questions

Q412

Mi hermano (WILL BE) doctor en tres años.

*Your Own Answer*_____

Q413

(IT IS) el primero de enero.

*Your Own Answer*_____

Q414

(IT WILL BE) tarde cuando llegamos.

*Your Own Answer*_____

Correct Answers

A412

SERÁ

A413

ES

A414

SERÁ

Questions

Q415

La fiesta (WAS) ayer.

Your Own Answer_____

Q416

La boda (WILL BE) en su iglesia favorita.

Your Own Answer_____

Q417

(IT WAS) menester hacerlo bien.

Your Own Answer_____

Correct Answers

A415

FUE

A416

SERÁ

A417

FUE/ERA

Questions

Q418

¿Dónde (HAVE YOU BEEN) tú?

*Your Own Answer*_____

Q419

Las ventanas (ARE) abiertas en el verano.

*Your Own Answer*_____

Q420

¿De dónde (ARE) sus vecinos?

*Your Own Answer*_____

Correct Answers

A418

HAS ESTADO

A419

ESTÁN

A420

SON

Questions

Q421

La fiesta (IS) aburrida; no hay nadie que me interese.

Your Own Answer_____

Q422

(IT WAS) lloviendo cuando llegaron.

Your Own Answer_____

Q423

La composición (IS) bien escrita.

Your Own Answer_____

Correct Answers

A421

ES

A422

ESTABA

A423

ESTÁ

Questions

Q424

Su hija (IS) callada; nunca dice nada.

*Your Own Answer*_____

Q425

Ese libro (WAS) escrito por Cervantes.

*Your Own Answer*_____

Q426

¿(ARE) listo, mi hijo? Debemos salir pronto.

*Your Own Answer*_____

Correct Answers

A424

ES

A425

FUE

A426

ESTÁS

Questions

Q427

Juana (HAS BEEN) triste desde que vio esa película.

*Your Own Answer*___

Q428

Yo (AM) débil porque no he comido en tres días.

*Your Own Answer*___

Q429

(IT HAS BEEN) posible hacer la tarea.

*Your Own Answer*___

Correct Answers

A427

HA ESTADO

A428

ESTOY

A429

HA SIDO

Questions

Q430

Los deportistas (ARE) débiles porque no han comido en tres días.

Your Own Answer___

Q431

El accidente (WAS) en la esquina, cerca de la tienda.

Your Own Answer___

Q432

Yo (WAS) dos noches en la selva.

Your Own Answer___

Correct Answers

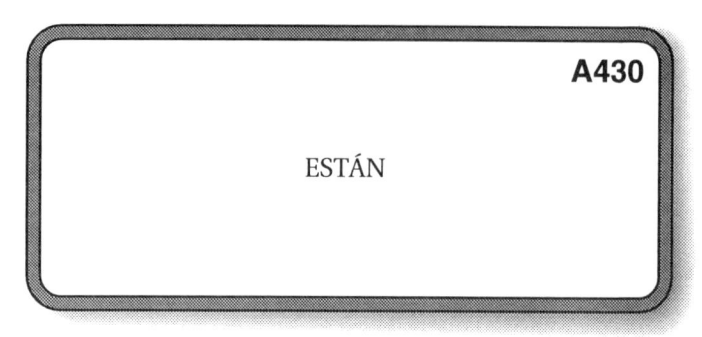

A430

ESTÁN

A431

FUE

A432

ESTUVE

Questions

Q433

La boda (WAS) en la iglesia.

Your Own Answer_____

Q434

Tú (WERE) equivocado cuando dijiste que no irías a la fiesta.

Your Own Answer_____

Q435

El padre de Alicia (IS) médico.

Your Own Answer_____

Correct Answers

A433

FUE

A434

ESTABAS

A435

ES

Questions

Q436

Los niños han (BEEN) tristes desde que sus padres murieron.

Your Own Answer_____

Q437

A verb used like a noun is called the _____.

Your Own Answer_____

Q438

In Spanish, the gerund is expressed using the____.

Your Own Answer_____

Correct Answers

A436

ESTADO

A437

gerund

A438

infinitive

Questions

Q439

In Spanish, a verb form following *seguir* or *continuar* is expressed using the _____ .

*Your Own Answer*_____

Q440

Verbs of perception (*ver, oír*) are commonly followed by the _____ in Spanish.

*Your Own Answer*_____

Q441

Verbs of motion (*ir, salir, entrar,* etc.) are commonly followed by the _____ in Spanish.

*Your Own Answer*_____

Correct Answers

A439

present participle

A440

infinitive

A441

present participle

Questions

Q442

The present participle (-ing form) of the verb in Spanish may never be used as a(n) _____ .

Your Own Answer_____

Q443

In Spanish, the verb form that follows a preposition must be the _____ .

Your Own Answer_____

Q444

Los oímos (SINGING).

Your Own Answer_____

Correct Answers

A442

adjective

A443

infinitive

A444

CANTAR

Questions

Q445

(RUNNING) es bueno para la salud.

Your Own Answer_____

Q446

Ver es (BELIEVING).

Your Own Answer_____

Q447

Continúan (REÍRSE) por mucho tiempo.

Your Own Answer_____

Correct Answers

A445

CORRER

A446

CREER

A447

RIÉNDOSE

Questions

Q448

Siga Ud. (CREER) la verdad.

*Your Own Answer*_____

Q449

Los chicos salieron (LLORAR).

*Your Own Answer*_____

Q450

Antes de (GOING), se puso el abrigo.

*Your Own Answer*_____

Correct Answers

A448

CREYENDO

A449

LLORANDO

A450

IR

Questions

Q451

El (CRYING CHILD) interrumpió el concierto.

Your Own Answer_____

Q452

Esto es (LIVING).

Your Own Answer_____

Q453

Al (HEARING) el ruido, se asustó.

Your Own Answer_____

Correct Answers

A451

NIÑO QUE LLORABA

A452

VIVIR

A453

OÍR

Questions

Q454

Lo que me gusta es (PLAYING) el piano.

*Your Own Answer*___

Q455

Vi a Juan (LEAVE).

*Your Own Answer*___

Q456

Seguiré (TO STUDY) el español.

*Your Own Answer*___

Correct Answers

A454

TOCAR

A455

SALIR

A456

ESTUDIANDO

Questions

Q457

Todos se fueron (CORRER).

*Your Own Answer*_____

Q458

El policía vio (ESCAPE) al ladrón.

*Your Own Answer*_____

Q459

Sin (BEING ABLE) ver bien, uno no puede conducir.

*Your Own Answer*_____

Correct Answers

A457

CORRIENDO

A458

ESCAPAR

A459

PODER

Questions

Q460

(SMOKING) cada día, se enfermó.

Your Own Answer_____

Q461

(WALKING) por la calle esta mañana, me caí.

Your Own Answer_____

Q462

(TELLING) la verdad es necesario en la iglesia.

Your Own Answer_____

Correct Answers

A460

FUMANDO

A461

ANDANDO

A462

DECIR

Questions

Q463

(HAVING EATEN) la comida, decidió pasearse.

*Your Own Answer*_____

Q464

Siguió hasta (ARRIVING) a la orilla.

*Your Own Answer*_____

Q465

Entró (CANTAR) porque estaba contento.

*Your Own Answer*_____

Correct Answers

A463

HABIENDO COMIDO

A464

LLEGAR

A465

CANTANDO

Questions

Q466

No puedo aguantar un (BARKING DOG).

Your Own Answer_____

Q467

To make a sentence negative in Spanish, place "no" _____ the verb.

Your Own Answer_____

Q468

Forms of the word _____ are used to make singular nouns negative.

Your Own Answer_____

Correct Answers

A466

PERRO QUE LADRA

A467

before

A468

ninguno

Questions

Q469

_____ and _____ are apocopated before masculine singular nouns.

Your Own Answer_____

Q470

To express "at all" with a noun use a singular form of _____ after the noun.

Your Own Answer_____

Q471

Algo difícil is translated as _____ .

Your Own Answer_____

Correct Answers

A469

Alguno; ninguno

A470

alguno

A471

somewhat difficult

Questions

Q472

The negative translation for "but" is _____ .

Your Own Answer _____

Q473

The forms of *ninguno* commonly used are _____ .

Your Own Answer _____

Q474

In a question expecting a negative answer, "ever" is expressed by _____ .

Your Own Answer _____

Correct Answers

A472

sino

A473

ningún, *ninguna,* and *ninguno*

A474

jamás

Questions

Q475

¿Recibiste una carta? No recibí (ANY).

*Your Own Answer*_____

Q476

(NONE) de los libros es mío.

*Your Own Answer*_____

Q477

(SOME DAY) voy a ser médico.

*Your Own Answer*_____

Correct Answers

A475

NINGUNA

A476

NINGUNO

A477

ALGÚN DÍA

Questions

Q478

No me gusta rojo, (BUT) azul.

Your Own Answer_____

Q479

Es necesario ir ahora (BUT) no quiero.

Your Own Answer_____

Q480

Lo hace mejor que (ANYONE).

Your Own Answer_____

Correct Answers

A478

SINO

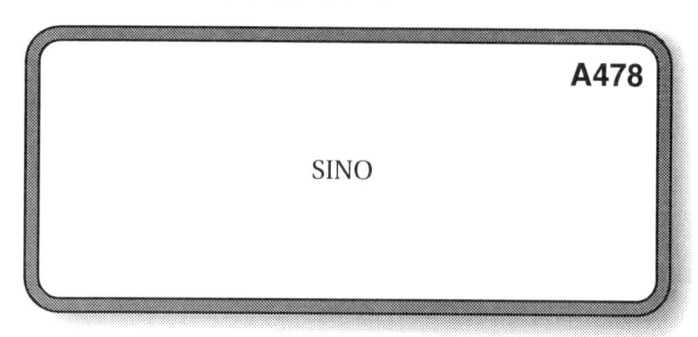

A479

PERO

A480

NADIE

Questions

Q481

Sin hablar con (ANYBODY), se fue.

Your Own Answer_____

Q482

(SOME) de las chicas han salido.

Your Own Answer_____

Q483

No veo a (ANYONE) en la sala.

Your Own Answer_____

Correct Answers

A481

NADIE

A482

ALGUNAS

A483

NADIE

Questions

Q484

Mas que (ANYTHING) quiero esquiar mañana.

Your Own Answer_____

Q485

Mas que (EVER) necesito ir a la fiesta.

Your Own Answer_____

Q486

No solo gana mucho dinero (BUT ALSO) gasta mucho.

Your Own Answer_____

Correct Answers

A484

NADA

A485

NUNCA

A486

SINO TAMBIÉN

Questions

Q487

Mi mamá (NO LONGER) tiene paciencia conmigo.

*Your Own Answer*_____

Q488

No me gusta la película ni mi novio (EITHER).

*Your Own Answer*_____

Q489

Sin hacer (ANYTHING) puede pasar los exámenes.

*Your Own Answer*_____

Correct Answers

A487

YA NO

A488

TAMPOCO

A489

NADA

Questions

Q490

¿Tiene ese hombre muchos amigos? No tiene (ANY).

*Your Own Answer*_____

Q491

¿Hay unas cartas en la mesa? No hay (ANY).

*Your Own Answer*_____

Q492

(NO) persona puede recordarlo todo.

*Your Own Answer*_____

Correct Answers

A490

NINGUNO

A491

NINGUNA

A492

NINGUNA

Questions

Q493

¿Has visto (EVER) tal cosa?

*Your Own Answer*_____

Q494

Pobre de Juan, no tiene (A FRIEND AT ALL).

*Your Own Answer*_____

Q495

(NO ONE) veo en el estadio.

*Your Own Answer*_____

Correct Answers

A493

JAMÁS

A494

AMIGO ALGUNO

A495

A NADIE

Questions

Q496

(NOT EVEN) su madre le visita.

Your Own Answer_____

Q497

No me gusta estudiar, (BUT) leer.

Your Own Answer_____

Q498

Ella no tiene dinero? (NOR HER FAMILY EITHER).

Your Own Answer_____

Correct Answers

A496

NI SIQUIERA

A497

SINO

A498

NI SU FAMILIA TAMPOCO

Questions

Q499

(NO) cantidad de dinero puede pagar la felicidad.

Your Own Answer_____

Q500

No se admite a (ANY GIRL) en esa universidad.

Your Own Answer_____

Q501

Possessive adjectives _____ the noun(s) they modify in Spanish.

Your Own Answer_____

Correct Answers

A499

NINGUNA

A500

NINGUNA CHICA

A501

precede

Questions

Q502

The possessive pronoun _____ the noun(s) it modifies.

Your Own Answer_____

Q503

Because in Spanish all possessive pronouns end in -o, there is a a total of _____ forms for each.

Your Own Answer_____

Q504

Normally with body parts or articles of clothing in Spanish the possessive adjective is replaced by the _____ .

Your Own Answer_____

Correct Answers

A502

replaces

A503

four

A504

definite article

Questions

Q505

The definite article in Spanish is omitted with the possessive pronoun commonly after the verb _____ .

*Your Own Answer*_____

Q506

¿De quién es este lápiz? Es (MINE).

*Your Own Answer*_____

Q507

¿De quién son estos zapatos? Son (MINE).

*Your Own Answer*_____

Correct Answers

A505

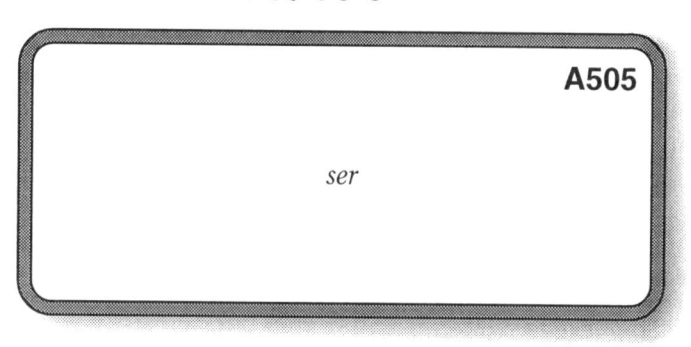

ser

A506

MÍO

A507

MÍOS

Questions

Q508

¿De quién es esta carta? Es (HIS).

Your Own Answer_____

Q509

Tu casa es más grande que (HERS).

Your Own Answer_____

Q510

Se quitó (HIS HAT) al entrar en la iglesia.

Your Own Answer_____

Correct Answers

A508

SUYA

A509

LA SUYA

A510

EL SOMBRERO

Questions

Q511

Varios (FRIENDS OF MINE) volaron a España.

*Your Own Answer*_____

Q512

Mi composición es mejor que (THEIRS).

*Your Own Answer*_____

Q513

(OUR) padres salieron en el fin de semana.

*Your Own Answer*_____

Correct Answers

A511

AMIGOS MÍOS

A512

LA SUYA

A513

NUESTROS

Questions

Q514

Un (UNCLE OF OURS) se casó recientemente.

*Your Own Answer*_____

Q515

¿Es (YOURS) esta pluma, mi hijo?

*Your Own Answer*_____

Q516

Su decisión y (THEIRS) son más importantes.

*Your Own Answer*_____

Correct Answers

A514

TÍO NUESTRO

A515

TUYA

A516

LA SUYA

Questions

Q517

¿Estas cajas? Son (HIS).

Your Own Answer_____

Q518

En (OUR) casa se prohibe fumar.

Your Own Answer_____

Q519

¿Las ideas? Son (HERS).

Your Own Answer_____

Correct Answers

A517

SUYAS

A518

NUESTRA

A519

SUYAS

Questions

Q520

¿Las respuestas? Son (HIS).

Your Own Answer_____

Q521

¡Dime (YOUR) opinión!

Your Own Answer_____

Q522

In Spanish a true passive verb form consists of a form of _____ and a _____ .

Your Own Answer_____

Correct Answers

A520

SUYAS

A521

TU

A522

"to be"; past participle

Questions

Q523

The past participle in English commonly ends in _____ unless it is irregular.

*Your Own Answer*_____

Q524

True or False: The agent in the statement is the doer of the action.

*Your Own Answer*_____

Q525

True or False: The past participle of the construction in Spanish has only two forms.

*Your Own Answer*_____

Correct Answers

A523

-ed

A524

False; the receiver

A525

False; up to four if it ends in -o

Questions

Q526

The past participle in Spanish is formed by adding _____ or _____ to the stem of the verb, if regular.

*Your Own Answer*_____

Q527

One can convert a passive statement to an active one by using the subject _____ .

*Your Own Answer*_____

Q528

Impersonal statements beginning with "one", "people", "they", and "you" are expressed in Spanish by _____ or simply the _____ of the verb.

*Your Own Answer*_____

Correct Answers

A526

-ado; -ido

A527

"they"

A528

SE + 3rd SINGULAR; 3rd PLURAL

Questions

Q529

La carta (IS WRITTEN) en español.

Your Own Answer_____

Q530

Mi casa (CONSTRUIR) por mi padre hace muchos años.

Your Own Answer_____

Q531

Aquí (HABLAR) español e inglés.

Your Own Answer_____

Correct Answers

A529

ESTÁ ESCRITA

A530

FUE CONSTRUIDA

A531

SE HABLA/HABLAN

Questions

Q532

(IT HAS BEEN SAID) que hay muchos terremotos allí.

Your Own Answer_____

Q533

Muchas cosas (ARE SOLD) en esa tienda.

Your Own Answer_____

Q534

Muchas ciudades (CONQUISTAR) por El Cid.

Your Own Answer_____

Correct Answers

A532

SE HA DICHO or HAN DICHO

A533

SE VENDEN

A534

FUERON CONQUISTADAS

Questions

Q535

(IT IS BELIEVED) que hay seres en otros planetas.

*Your Own Answer*_____

Q536

En este autobús (YOU PAY) al subir.

*Your Own Answer*_____

Q537

(PEOPLE THINK) que el español es fácil.

*Your Own Answer*_____

Correct Answers

A535

SE CREE or CREEN

A536

SE PAGA or PAGAN

A537

SE CREE or CREEN

Questions

Q538

Juana (IS LOVED) por todos.

*Your Own Answer*_____

Q539

Ese desfile (VER) por todos el primero de enero.

*Your Own Answer*_____

Q540

Puedo ver que las ventanas (ARE OPENED).

*Your Own Answer*_____

Correct Answers

A538

ES AMADA

A539

FUE VISTO

A540

ESTÁN ABIERTAS

Questions

Q541

(IT IS NOT KNOWN) si él regresará.

*Your Own Answer*_____

Q542

Muchos cuentos (HAVE BEEN WRITTEN) por mi clase más avanzada.

*Your Own Answer*_____

Q543

(PROHIBIR) fumar en cualquier escuela.

*Your Own Answer*_____

Correct Answers

A541

NO SE SABE or NO SABEN

A542

HAN SIDO ESCRITOS

A543

SE PROHIBE

Questions

Q544

¿A dónde (DOES ONE GO) para comprar pan?

*Your Own Answer*___

Q545

(ONE CAN SEE) que es imposible ganar.

*Your Own Answer*___

Q546

(DECIRSE) que va a mejorar la economía.

*Your Own Answer*___

Correct Answers

A544

SE VA

A545

SE PUEDE VER

A546

SE DICE

Questions

Q547

La señora Martínez es respetada _____ todos.

*Your Own Answer*_____

Q548

Aquí (HABLARSE) español.

*Your Own Answer*_____

Q549

Mi casa fue (BUILT) por mi abuelo.

*Your Own Answer*_____

Correct Answers

A547

por

A548

SE HABLA

A549

CONSTRUIDA

Questions

Q550

Al acercarme a la casa vi que la puerta (WAS) abierta.

*Your Own Answer*_____

Q551

True or False: The direct and indirect object pronouns in Spanish are exactly alike.

*Your Own Answer*_____

Q552

True or False: When two pronouns are used with the verb form, the direct object pronoun will be first.

*Your Own Answer*_____

Correct Answers

A550

ESTABA

A551

False; they differ in the third singular and plural forms.

A552

False; the indirect object always precedes the direct object pronoun.

Questions

Q553

The indirect object pronoun (*le/les*) becomes *se* when _____ .

Your Own Answer_____

Q554

True or False: An accent mark is required on the infinitive whenever any pronoun is attached.

Your Own Answer_____

Q555

True or False: Object pronouns cannot be attached to the past participle.

Your Own Answer_____

Correct Answers

A553

it/they precede a direct object pronoun that begins with "l" (i.e. lo, la, los, las)

A554

False; only when two pronouns are attached

A555

True; only to the present participle

Questions

Q556

True or False: Direct object and indirect object pronouns are attached to conjugated verbs.

Your Own Answer_____

Q557

Prepositional pronouns are duplicates of the _____ pronouns except for *mí*, *tí*, and *sí*.

Your Own Answer_____

Q558

Con combines with *mí*, *tí*, and *sí* to become _____, _____, and _____ .

Your Own Answer_____

Correct Answers

A556

False; they precede

A557

subject

A558

conmigo; contigo; consigo

Questions

Q559

Entre, salvo, menos, excepto, and según are followed by _____ pronouns.

Your Own Answer_____

Q560

Quieren dar (IT TO ME).

Your Own Answer_____

Q561

¡Traiga (THEM TO US)!

Your Own Answer_____

Correct Answers

A559

subject or personal

A560

DÁRMELO

A561

¡TRÁIGANOSLOS!

Questions

Q562

Estaba enviando (THEM TO HER).

*Your Own Answer*_____

Q563

Después de (HAVING SEEN HER), se fue para siempre.

*Your Own Answer*_____

Q564

Leyendo (IT TO HER), se durmió.

*Your Own Answer*_____

Correct Answers

A562

ENVIÁNDOSELOS A ELLA

A563

HABERLA VISTO

A564

LEYÉNDOSELO A ELLA

Questions

Q565

Tiene tres libros nuevos. Dé (THEM TO HIM).

Your Own Answer_____

Q566

No (SING IT TO US) hasta que llegue el coro. [la canción]

Your Own Answer_____

Q567

Vete a la puerta porque detrás de (IT) hay un armario.

Your Own Answer_____

Correct Answers

A565

DÉSELOS A ÉL

A566

NOS LA CANTE

A567

ELLA

Questions

Q568

A pesar de (THEM), voy a la fiesta.

*Your Own Answer*_____

Q569

Entre (YOU AND ME), mi amigo, no lo creo.

*Your Own Answer*_____

Q570

Primero debes hallar la caja y en (IT) verás las joyas.

*Your Own Answer*_____

Correct Answers

A568

ELLOS

A569

TÚ Y YO

A570

ELLA

Questions

Q571

(I SAW HER) entrar por esa puerta.

*Your Own Answer*_____

Q572

¿Sabes que ella se casó ayer? Sí, (I KNOW).

*Your Own Answer*_____

Q573

¡Ven (TO ME), Paco!

*Your Own Answer*_____

Correct Answers

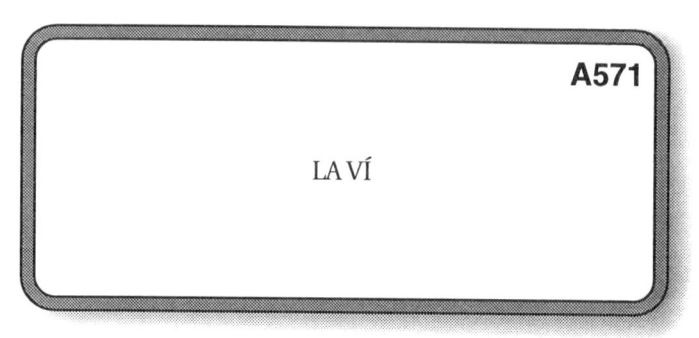

A571

LA VÍ

A572

LO SÉ

A573

A MÍ

Questions

Q574

¿Quién es? (IT IS I).

Your Own Answer_____

Q575

Ella (GAVE HIM) un regalo muy caro.

Your Own Answer_____

Q576

Estas flores son (FOR YOU), mi amor.

Your Own Answer_____

Correct Answers

A574

SOY YO

A575

LE DIÓ

A576

PARA TÍ

Questions

Q577

María me dijo un secreto; _____ dijo el otro día.

*Your Own Answer*_____

Q578

Invité a Carmen a que fuera (WITH ME).

*Your Own Answer*_____

Q579

Mi novio quería casarse conmigo pero nunca _____ dijo.

*Your Own Answer*_____

Correct Answers

A577

me lo

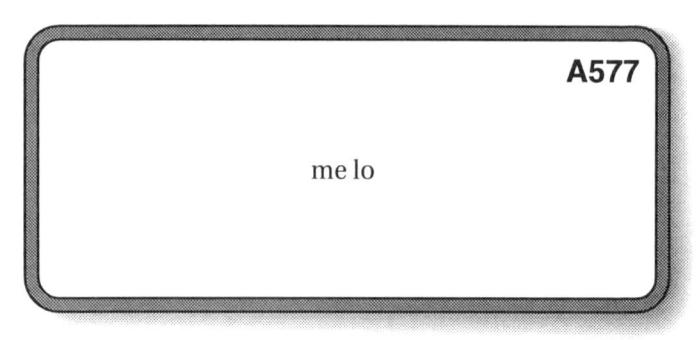

A578

CONMIGO

A579

me lo

Questions

Q580

Pablo no entendía los pronombres: el profesor _____ explicó a él.

Your Own Answer_____

Q581

María es muy bella. Ayer _____ vi.

Your Own Answer_____

Q582

Ella _____ un regalo a su hermano.

Your Own Answer_____

Correct Answers

A580

se los

A581

la

A582

le dió

Questions

Q583

Todos van a la fiesta menos (ME).

Your Own Answer___

Q584

Ella siempre _____ esconde su dinero de mi madre y de mí.

Your Own Answer___

Q585

No puedo hallar mis llaves; tengo que (LOOK FOR THEM).

Your Own Answer___

Correct Answers

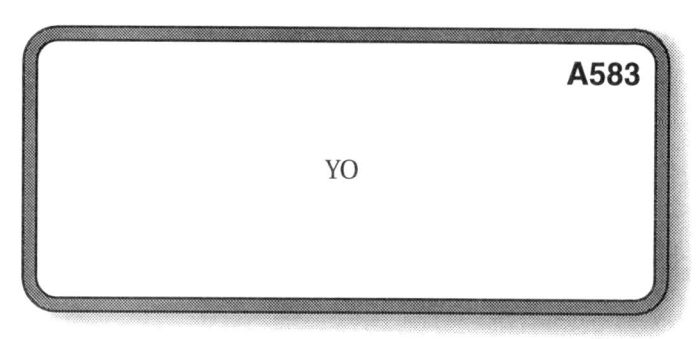

A583

YO

A584

nos

A585

BUSCARLAS

Questions

Q586

Fué horrible; no quiero pensar en (IT).

*Your Own Answer*_____

Q587

El reo ha escapado; yo mismo _____ vi.

*Your Own Answer*_____

Q588

A los niños _____ dieron los premios.

*Your Own Answer*_____

Correct Answers

A586

ELLO

A587

LO or LE

A588

les

Questions

Q589

Aquí tienes la ropa nueva; debes (WEAR IT).

*Your Own Answer*_____

Q590

Hallé la calle principal, al lado de (IT) hay unos edificios importantes.

*Your Own Answer*_____

Q591

Necesito saber la verdad, señor. (TELL IT TO ME)!

*Your Own Answer*_____

Correct Answers

A589

PONERLA

A590

ELLA

A591

¡DÍGAMELA!

Questions

Q592

Al chico _____ regalaron el dinero.

*Your Own Answer*_____

Q593

Tú tienes una deuda muy grande; debes (PAY IT TO ME) dentro de poco.

*Your Own Answer*_____

Q594

Tú tienes mi coche y en (IT) he puesto las llaves.

*Your Own Answer*_____

Correct Answers

A592

le

A593

PAGÁRMELA

A594

ÉL

Questions

Q595

Aquí está su escritorio; ¡(UNDER IT) ponga sus libros!

*Your Own Answer*_____

Q596

(LET'S NOT GO) hasta que lleguen.

*Your Own Answer*_____

Q597

(I HOPE I CAN) leer la carta bien.

*Your Own Answer*_____

Correct Answers

A595

DEBAJO DE ÉL

A596

NO NOS VAYAMOS

A597

ESPERO PODER

Questions

Q598

No había ningún libro que (WAS WRITTEN) por Fuentes.

Your Own Answer___

Q599

(NO MATTER HOW NECESSARY THEY ARE), no voy a comprarlos.

Your Own Answer___

Q600

Le rogué a Ben que (LEAVE) temprano.

Your Own Answer___

Correct Answers

A598

FUERA ESCRITO

A599

POR NECESARIOS QUE SEAN

A600

SALIERA

Questions

Q601

¡(LET THEM DEMAND) el dinero!

Your Own Answer_____

Q602

Ha como si (HE KNEW) al actor bien.

Your Own Answer_____

Q603

A menos que (WE FIND) las llaves, no iremos.

Your Own Answer_____

Correct Answers

A601

QUE EXIJAN

A602

CONOCIERAS

A603

HALLEMOS or ENCONTREMOS

Questions

Q604

Si (I SEE) la película, te invitaré a ir.

*Your Own Answer*_____

Q605

Es importante que (WE CONTINUE) haciéndolo.

*Your Own Answer*_____

Q606

(WITHOUT MY DOING) nada, me lo confesó.

*Your Own Answer*_____

Correct Answers

A604

VEO

A605

CONTINUEMOS

A606

SIN QUE HICIERA

Questions

Q607

(DO WHAT YOU WILL), no voy a pagar.

Your Own Answer_____

Q608

(SAY WHAT YOU WILL), no iré contigo.

Your Own Answer_____

Q609

(NO MATTER WHAT HAPPENS), te amaré.

Your Own Answer_____

Correct Answers

A607

HAGA LO QUE HAGA

A608

DIGAS LO QUE DIGAS

A609

PASE LO QUE PASE

Questions

Q610

(WHOEVER HE IS), no lo dejé entrar.

*Your Own Answer*_____

Q611

Dígale a Juana (TO SHUT UP).

*Your Own Answer*_____

Q612

Clauses beginning with "as if" must be followed by the _____ in Spanish.

*Your Own Answer*_____

Correct Answers

A610

QUIENQUIERA QUE SEA

A611

QUE SE CALLE

A612

past subjunctive

Questions

Q613

Adjective clauses modify nouns technically called _____ .

*Your Own Answer*_____

Q614

True or False: An "if clause" may contain both the -re or -se forms of the subjunctive.

*Your Own Answer*_____

Q615

True or False: If the "if clause" contains a past subjunctive, the independent clause may also contain one.

*Your Own Answer*_____

Correct Answers

A613

antecedents

A614

True

A615

True

Questions

Q616

The most common relative pronoun used to introduce a noun clause is _____.

Your Own Answer_____

Q617

The most common relative pronoun used to introduce an adjective clause is _____.

Your Own Answer_____

Q618

For an adjective clause to contain a subjunctive verb, the antecedent it modifies must be _____ or _____.

Your Own Answer_____

Correct Answers

A616

que

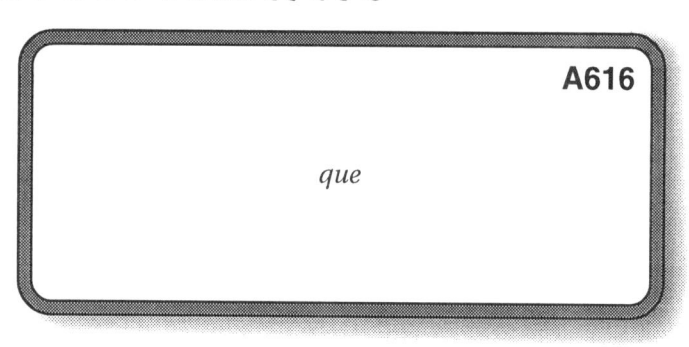

A617

que

A618

negative; indefinite

Questions

Q619

No estoy segura pero tal vez ella (REGRESAR).

*Your Own Answer*_____

Q620

Si yo hubiera comprado el regalo, yo te lo (DAR).

*Your Own Answer*_____

Q621

Mi mamá quería que yo (HACER) la cama.

*Your Own Answer*_____

Correct Answers

A619

REGRESE

A620

HUBIERA DADO

A621

HICIERA

Questions

Q622

Habla como si (SER) mi mejor amiga.

Your Own Answer_____

Q623

Es obvio que los niños no (ESTAR) en sus cuartos durmiendo.

Your Own Answer_____

Q624

Por bien que (JUGAR), Juan no va a ir con nosotros.

Your Own Answer_____

Correct Answers

A622

FUERA

A623

ESTÁN

A624

JUEGUE

Questions

Q625

Mi padre me dió dinero para que yo (TENER) lo que necesitaba.

*Your Own Answer*_____

Q626

No vendrías si (ENTENDER) la situación.

*Your Own Answer*_____

Q627

Si te (DAR) un beso, ¿qué harás?

*Your Own Answer*_____

Correct Answers

A625

TUVIERA

A626

ENTENDIERAS or ENTENDIESES

A627

DOY

Questions

Q628

No creo que mis amigos me (HAVE LEFT).

*Your Own Answer*_____

Q629

Nos pidió que (SALIR) temprano.

*Your Own Answer*_____

Q630

Ellos pueden participar con tal que (PAGAR) la cuenta.

*Your Own Answer*_____

Correct Answers

A628

HAYAN DEJADO

A629

SALIÉRAMOS

A630

PAGUEN

Questions

Q631

El cartero dice que mis vecinos (RECIBIR) muchas cartas.

*Your Own Answer*_____

Q632

No había nadie que (LEER) sin problemas.

*Your Own Answer*_____

Q633

Lo harán cuando me (VER).

*Your Own Answer*_____

Correct Answers

A631

RECIBEN

A632

LEYERA

A633

VEAN

Questions

Q634

Se lo mandaré si (TENER) libre tiempo.

*Your Own Answer*_____

Q635

Cuando quieras que (IR), dímelo.

*Your Own Answer*_____

Q636

Busco el libro que (CONTENER) la información sobre la guerra.

*Your Own Answer*_____

Correct Answers

A634

TENGO

A635

VAYA

A636

CONTIENE

Questions

Q637

No es dudoso que (LLOVER) ahora.

*Your Own Answer*_____

Q638

Nos alegramos de que él (HAS RETURNED).

*Your Own Answer*_____

Q639

¿Deseas (VIAJAR) por avión?

*Your Own Answer*_____

Correct Answers

A637

LLUEVE

A638

HAYA REGRESADO

A639

VIAJAR

Questions

Q640

¡Ojalá que no (HABER) un terremoto!

*Your Own Answer*_____

Q641

Fue lástima que ella no (PODER) contar contigo.

*Your Own Answer*_____

Q642

Te suplico que (TO BRING) los discos.

*Your Own Answer*_____

Correct Answers

A640

HAYA

A641

PUDIERA

A642

TRAIGAS

Questions

Q643

En caso de que (HACER) mal tiempo, vamos a reunirnos en casa.

*Your Own Answer*___

Q644

Les aconsejé a los adultos que no (REÍRSE).

*Your Own Answer*___

Q645

Cada día cuando (VOLVER) a casa, lavo los platos.

*Your Own Answer*___

Correct Answers

A643

HAGA

A644

SE RIERAN

A645

VUELVO

Questions

Q646

¿Conoce Ud. a alguien que (BAILAR) bien?

*Your Own Answer*_____

Q647

Me miró como si ella (HAD SEEN) a un fantasma.

*Your Own Answer*_____

Q648

Busca una casa que (ESTAR) cerca del mar.

*Your Own Answer*_____

Correct Answers

A646

BAILE

A647

HUBIERA VISTO

A648

ESTÉ

Questions

Q649

Antes de que tú (SIT DOWN), habla conmigo.

Your Own Answer_____

Q650

Juan ve un traje que (HE LIKES).

Your Own Answer_____

Q651

Si (HACER) buen tiempo, iría a la playa.

Your Own Answer_____

Correct Answers

A649

TE SIENTES

A650

LE GUSTA

A651

HICIERA/HICIESE

Questions

Q652

Encontramos un buen restaurante donde (SERVIR) buena comida.

*Your Own Answer*_____

_____

Q653

Si van a la playa, (DIVERTIRSE).

*Your Own Answer*_____

_____

Q654

(YOU SHOULD) visitar a tu mamá.

*Your Own Answer*_____

_____

Correct Answers

A652

SIRVEN

A653

SE DIVERTIRÁN

A654

DEBES

Questions

Q655

En caso de que (NECESITAR) una pluma, préstele la mía.

*Your Own Answer*___

Q656

No había nada en la tienda que me (INTERESAR).

*Your Own Answer*___

Q657

Voy a comprar el reloj aunque (SUBIR) el precio.

*Your Own Answer*___

Correct Answers

A655

NECESITE

A656

INTERESARA

A657

SUBA

Questions

Q658

Devolvió el libro sin que yo lo (LEER).

*Your Own Answer*_____

Q659

Condujo el coche nuevo a casa para que su esposa lo (VER).

*Your Own Answer*_____

Q660

Quienquiera que (LLAMAR), no abras la puerta.

*Your Own Answer*_____

Correct Answers

A658

LEYERA

A659

VIERA

A660

LLAME

Questions

Q661

Me esperaron hasta que yo (LLEGAR).

Your Own Answer_____

Q662

No hay ninguna mujer aquí que (SABER) mi número de teléfono.

Your Own Answer_____

Q663

Cenaremos antes de que Uds. (MARCHARSE).

Your Own Answer_____

Correct Answers

A661

LLEGUÉ

A662

SEPA

A663

SE MARCHEN

Questions

Q664

En mi oficina no había ningún hombre que (ASISTIR) a la universidad.

*Your Own Answer*_____

Q665

Me aconsejaron que no (SEGUIR) esta ruta.

*Your Own Answer*_____

Q666

Cualquier libro que los niños (ESCOGER), lo van a leer.

*Your Own Answer*_____

Correct Answers

A664

ASISTIERA

A665

SIGUIERA

A666

ESCOJAN

Questions

Q667

Si tengo el dinero, te lo (MANDAR).

*Your Own Answer*_____

Q668

Ella quiere que yo le (MOSTAR) la información.

*Your Own Answer*_____

Q669

Voy a hallar la mujer que (TENER) mi licencia.

*Your Own Answer*_____

Correct Answers

A667

MANDARÉ

A668

MUESTRE

A669

TIENE

Questions

Q670

Me dijo que lo haría cuando (VOLVER).

Your Own Answer_____

Q671

Habla como si (SER) mi padre.

Your Own Answer_____

Q672

Yo conozco a un señor que (HABLAR) seis idiomas.

Your Own Answer_____

Correct Answers

A670

VOLVIERA

A671

FUERA

A672

HABLA

Questions

Q673

Te lo dirán cuando te (VISITAR).

*Your Own Answer*_____

Q674

Si hubiera sabido eso, no lo (HACER).

*Your Own Answer*_____

Q675

¿(DO THEY KNOW) esa ciudad bien?

*Your Own Answer*_____

Correct Answers

A673

VISITEN

A674

HABRÍA HECHO

A675

CONOCEN

Questions

Q676

¿(DID HE MEET) a su novia el año pasado?

*Your Own Answer*___

Q677

¿(DOES SHE KNOW) a sus parientes de España?

*Your Own Answer*___

Q678

(I DON'T KNOW HOW) jugar al ajedrez.

*Your Own Answer*___

Correct Answers

A676

CONOCIÓ

A677

CONOCE ELLA

A678

NO SÉ

Questions

Q679

Todos (FOUND OUT) que se fue temprano.

*Your Own Answer*_____

Q680

Espero que tú (KNOW) la dirección.

*Your Own Answer*_____

Q681

Ojalá que (THEY LEAVE) a María en el hospital.

*Your Own Answer*_____

Correct Answers

A679

SUPIERON

A680

SEPAS

A681

DEJEN

Questions

Q682

(SPENDING) tiempo en el campo es bueno para el alma.

*Your Own Answer*_____

Q683

Espero que mi esposa no (SPEND) más de lo que gana.

*Your Own Answer*_____

Q684

¿Quién (PLAYED) el piano en el concierto anoche?

*Your Own Answer*_____

Correct Answers

A682

PASAR

A683

GASTE

A684

TOCÓ

Questions

Q685

Ella le (ASKED) al mozo el menú.

*Your Own Answer*_____

Q686

En un mes yo (WILL TAKE) un tren para ir a Madrid.

*Your Own Answer*_____

Q687

Juan me (ASKED) a dónde voy.

*Your Own Answer*_____

Correct Answers

A685

PIDIÓ

A686

TOMARÉ

A687

PREGUNTÓ

Questions

Q688

Es importante que los alumnos (RETURN) los libros a tiempo.

Your Own Answer_____

Q689

No puedo ver a Juan a menos que (HE RETURNS) dentro de poco.

Your Own Answer_____

Q690

Ella (BECAME) triste al ver a su padre enfermo.

Your Own Answer_____

Correct Answers

A688

DEVUELVAN

A689

VUELVA

A690

SE PUSO

Questions

Q691

Ella no (REALIZED) que alguien le robó la cartera.

*Your Own Answer*_____

Q692

Es dudoso que mi hermana (REALIZE) su sueño de ser doctora.

*Your Own Answer*_____

Q693

Raúl (BECAME) abogado después de muchos años de estudiar.

*Your Own Answer*_____

Correct Answers

A691

SE DIO CUENTA DE

A692

REALICE

A693

SE HIZO

Questions

Q694

Yo siempre (MISS) el tren cuando me despierto tarde.

*Your Own Answer*_____

Q695

Luisa (MISSES) a su familia cuando regresa a la universidad cada año.

*Your Own Answer*_____

Q696

Nadie (ENJOYS) estudiando los fines de semana.

*Your Own Answer*_____

Correct Answers

A694

PIERDO

A695

ECHA DE MENOS or EXTRANA

A696

GOZA or DISFRUTA

Questions

Q697

Tiene que (KEEP) sus joyas en la caja fuerte.

Your Own Answer_____

Q698

No hay nadie que (SAVES) todo su dinero.

Your Own Answer_____

Q699

¿Por qué no (WORK) el coche cuando tengo poco dinero?

Your Own Answer_____

Correct Answers

A697

GUARDAR

A698

AHORRE

A699

FUNCIONA

Questions

Q700

Nunca debes (WORK) los domingos.

*Your Own Answer*_____

Q701

El año pasado ellos (MOVED) a Nueva York.

*Your Own Answer*_____

Q702

¿Quién (MOVED) mi máquina de escribir?

*Your Own Answer*_____

Correct Answers

A700

TRABAJAR

A701

SE MUDARON

A702

MOVIÓ

Questions

Q703

Ella (ATTENDED) a esta escuela el año pasado.

Your Own Answer_____

Q704

Mi padre (SMELLS) a sudor después de un día largo de trabajo.

Your Own Answer_____

Q705

Al subir al tren, Juan (SAID GOOD-BYE) de sus parientes.

Your Own Answer_____

Correct Answers

A703

ASISTIÓ

A704

HUELE

A705

SE DESPIDIÓ

Questions

Q706

El atleta terminó la carrera sin (BREATH).

*Your Own Answer*_____

Q707

No debes (LEAN AGAINST) en esta pared; vas a caerte.

*Your Own Answer*_____

Q708

No se (REMEMBER) de nada después de sufrir un examen muy difícil.

*Your Own Answer*_____

Correct Answers

A706

ALIENTO

A707

APOYARTE

A708

ACUERDA

Questions

Q709

En la arena uno puede (SUNBATHE).

*Your Own Answer*____

Q710

El collar es (OF PEARLS).

*Your Own Answer*____

Q711

(BECAUSE) estuvimos cansados, descansamos.

*Your Own Answer*____

Correct Answers

A709

TOMAR EL SOL

A710

DE PERLAS

A711

COMO

Questions

Q712

(BECAUSE OF) la nieve, no pudo conducir bien.

*Your Own Answer*_____

Q713

Todos los (CHARACTERS) de esta novela están muertos.

*Your Own Answer*_____

Q714

El éxito de la elección depende del (CHARACTER) del candidato.

*Your Own Answer*_____

Correct Answers

A712

A CAUSA DE or POR

A713

PERSONAJES

A714

CARACTER

Questions

Q715

Después de dos meses su matrimonio (FAILED).

Your Own Answer_____

Q716

Cuando el motor (FAILED) tuvimos que arreglar nuestro coche.

Your Own Answer_____

Q717

El cura (MARRIED) la pareja.

Your Own Answer_____

Correct Answers

A715

FRACASÓ

A716

FALLÓ

A717

CASÓ A

Questions

Q718

La pareja (GOT MARRIED) el sábado pasado.

Your Own Answer____

Q719

Juan (MARRIED) Isabel el año pasado.

Your Own Answer____

Q720

Debemos leer el (PAPER) cada día.

Your Own Answer____

Correct Answers

A718

SE CASÓ

A719

SE CASÓ CON

A720

PERIÓDICO

Questions

Q721

El (PAPER) cuesta mucho hoy en día.

*Your Own Answer*_____

Q722

María (IS RIGHT) todo el tiempo.

*Your Own Answer*_____

Q723

Siga (TO THE RIGHT) por esta calle.

*Your Own Answer*_____

Correct Answers

A721

PAPEL

A722

TIENE RAZÓN

A723

A LA DERECHA

Questions

Q724

Todos tienen (THE RIGHT) de votar.

*Your Own Answer*_____

Q725

No tengo (TIME) para leerlo todo.

*Your Own Answer*_____

Q726

¿Qué (TIME) es?

*Your Own Answer*_____

Correct Answers

A724

EL DERECHO

A725

TIEMPO

A726

HORA

Questions

Q727

(THIS TIME) voy sola al cine.

*Your Own Answer*_____

Q728

(AT THIS TIME) no tengo respuesta.

*Your Own Answer*_____

Q729

Un sinónimo de HAY QUE es _____.

*Your Own Answer*_____

Correct Answers

A727

ESTA VEZ

A728

EN ESTE MOMENTO

A729

ES MENESTER or ES NECESARIO

Questions

Q730

Un sinónimo de ESTAR A PUNTO DE es _____.

Your Own Answer_____

Q731

Un sinónimo de NO OBSTANTE es _____.

Your Own Answer_____

Q732

Un sinónimo de ECHARSE A es _____.

Your Own Answer_____

Correct Answers

A730

ESTAR PARA

A731

SIN EMBARGO

A732

PONERSE A

Questions

Q733

In any sentence requiring the subjunctive, the subjunctive verb will occur in the _____ clause.

*Your Own Answer*_____

Q734

Dudo que el cajero (TRAERME) la carta que espero hoy.

*Your Own Answer*_____

Q735

Me parece que tú (PAGAR) demasiado por tu traje nuevo.

*Your Own Answer*_____

Correct Answers

A733

dependent

A734

ME TRAIGA

A735

PAGASTE

Questions

Q736

No me parece que (LLOVER) ahora.

*Your Own Answer*_____

Q737

Mi mamá dice que su abrigo (IS) de lana pura.

*Your Own Answer*_____

Q738

Necesito un abrigo que (IS) de pura lana.

*Your Own Answer*_____

Correct Answers

A736

LLUEVA

A737

ES

A738

SEA

Questions

Q739

¿Hay alguien aquí que (KNOWS) mi dirección?

Your Own Answer_____

Q740

No hay nadie que (HAS WORKED) con el nuevo presidente.

Your Own Answer_____

Q741

Dudamos que esa casa (HAS) agua corriente.

Your Own Answer_____

Correct Answers

A739

SEPA

A740

HAYA TRABAJADO

A741

TENGA

Questions

Q742

Antes de que Juanita (RETURNS), hábleme.

*Your Own Answer*_____

Q743

A menos que yo (EARN) más dinero, no puedo pagar el alquiler.

*Your Own Answer*_____

Q744

¡Ojalá que (HE TRANSLATES) bien!

*Your Own Answer*_____

Correct Answers

A742

VUELVA

A743

GANE

A744

TRADUZCA

Questions

Q745

Si ellos (TENER) el dinero, me pagarán.

Your Own Answer_____

Q746

Si ellos (RECIBIR) el dinero, me pagarían.

Your Own Answer_____

Q747

Si ellos hubieran enviado la cuenta, yo la (PAGAR).

Your Own Answer_____

Correct Answers

A745

TIENEN

A746

RECIBIERAN

A747

HABRÍA PAGADO

Questions

Q748

¡Que la maestra (MOSTRAR) la información!

Your Own Answer___

Q749

(LET'S SIT DOWN) en este rincón. [one word]

Your Own Answer___

Q750

¡(LET'S STAND UP) en sequida! [one word]

Your Own Answer___

Correct Answers

A748

MUESTRE

A749

SENTÉMONOS

A750

LEVANTÉMONOS

Questions

Q751

Me gustaba que mi mamá (DECIR) esas cosas.

*Your Own Answer*_____

Q752

Quería hallar una secretaria que (ENTENDER) más de un idioma.

*Your Own Answer*_____

Q753

Sabemos que algo excitante (HAS) ocurrido.

*Your Own Answer*_____

Correct Answers

A751

DIJERA

A752

ENTENDIERA

A753

HA

Questions

Q754

Será necesario que ellos (ELECT) a un alcalde.

*Your Own Answer*_____

Q755

Me aconsejó que yo (USE) el subjuntivo.

*Your Own Answer*_____

Q756

Colón negó que el mundo (SER) llano.

*Your Own Answer*_____

Correct Answers

A754

ELIJAN

A755

USARA

A756

FUERA

Questions

Q757

Por rico que (SER), no le prestaría nada.

Your Own Answer_____

Q758

El juez no le creyó aunque él (SAID) la verdad.

Your Own Answer_____

Q759

No hay nada que (VALER) la pena.

Your Own Answer_____

Correct Answers

A757

FUERA

A758

DIJO

A759

VALGA

Questions

Q760

Habla como si lo (SABER) todo.

*Your Own Answer*_____

Q761

Este es el único empleado que (SABER) escribir bien.

*Your Own Answer*_____

Q762

Necesito volver antes de que mis padres (REGRESAR).

*Your Own Answer*_____

Correct Answers

A760

SUPIERA

A761

SABE

A762

REGRESEN

Questions

Q763

Haría el viaje si (TENER) el dinero.

Your Own Answer_____

Q764

El profesor dio un breve discurso antes de (LEER).

Your Own Answer_____

Q765

No puedo ponerme el traje de baño a menos que (BAJAR) de peso.

Your Own Answer_____

Correct Answers

A763

TUVIERA

A764

LEER

A765

BAJE

Questions

Q766

Si Juan (ENTENDER) el problema, podrá resolvero.

*Your Own Answer*_____

Q767

Hicimos el viaje tan pronto como (TENER) el dinero.

*Your Own Answer*_____

Q768

Es cierto que Marta (WON) el premio gordo.

*Your Own Answer*_____

Correct Answers

A766

ENTIENDE

A767

TUVIMOS

A768

GANÓ

Questions

Q769

Después que todos (LLEGAR), se cerraron las puertas.

*Your Own Answer*_____

Q770

When referring to a person after a preposition only _____ or _____ may be used in Spanish.

*Your Own Answer*_____

Q771

True or False: The phrase "that which" (what) may be expressed using either *lo que* or *lo cual*.

*Your Own Answer*_____

Correct Answers

A769

LLEGARON

A770

quien; quienes

A771

FALSE; only lo que

Questions

Q772

Commonly before a noun, "whose" is expressed in Spanish using the corresponding form of _____.

*Your Own Answer*_____

Q773

Los señores de (WHOM) hablo, son hermanos.

*Your Own Answer*_____

Q774

Marta, (WHOSE) hija es médica, acaba de salir.

*Your Own Answer*_____

Correct Answers

A772

cuyo

A773

QUIENES

A774

CUYA

Questions

Q775

(HE WHO) come bien, vive bien.

*Your Own Answer*_____

Q776

El padre de Julia, (WHO) es profesor, me invitó a la fiesta.

*Your Own Answer*_____

Q777

La madre de Raúl, (WHO) es médica, acaba de graduarse.

*Your Own Answer*_____

Correct Answers

A775

EL QUE or QUIEN

A776

QUIEN

A777

LA QUE or LA CUAL

Questions

Q778

(WHAT) mi amigo dijo es verdad.

*Your Own Answer*_____

Q779

Los alumnos siempre llegan tarde, (WHICH) no me gusta.

*Your Own Answer*_____

Q780

La puerta, (THROUGH WHICH) entraron los invitados, es de acero fino.

*Your Own Answer*_____

Correct Answers

A778

LO QUE

A779

LO QUE or LO CUAL

A780

POR LA QUE or POR LA CUAL

Questions

Q781

Aquí tienes la información (WITHOUT WHICH) no podrás salir bien.

*Your Own Answer*_____

Q782

Acérquese a esa puerta (BEHIND WHICH) va a encontrar el armario.

*Your Own Answer*_____

Q783

El lago era hondo, (WHICH) me inspiró terror.

*Your Own Answer*_____

Correct Answers

A781

SIN LA QUE or SIN LA CUAL

A782

DETRÁS DE LA QUE or DETRAS DE LA CUAL

A783

LO CUAL

Questions

Q784

De nuevo mencioné _____ había mencionado antes.

*Your Own Answer*_____

Q785

La bicicleta de Raúl, _____ es nueva, se le rompió.

*Your Own Answer*_____

Q786

_____ estudia, aprende mucho.

*Your Own Answer*_____

Correct Answers

A784

lo que

A785

la cual/la que

A786

Quien/El que

Questions

Q787

¿Conoces a esos hombres con _____ Anita acaba de hablar?

Your Own Answer_____

Q788

Mi hija habla bien el español, (WHICH) es bueno.

Your Own Answer_____

Q789

En aquel castillo hay grandes ventanas por _____ se ven las montañas.

Your Own Answer_____

Correct Answers

A787

quienes/los que

A788

LO CUAL

A789

las que/las cuales

Questions

Q790

The difference between the demonstrative adjectives and pronouns in Spanish is that the pronouns _____.

*Your Own Answer*_____

Q791

To express "the latter" in Spanish, forms of _____ are used.

*Your Own Answer*_____

Q792

To express "the former" in Spanish forms of _____ are used.

*Your Own Answer*_____

Correct Answers

A790

have accent marks

A791

éste

A792

aquél

Questions

Q793

Demonstrative pronouns that end in -o are _____.

Your Own Answer _____

Q794

When referring to something that is "far from" both the speaker and the listener, forms of _____ are used before the noun.

Your Own Answer _____

Q795

¿Qué es (THIS)? No entiendo.

Your Own Answer _____

Correct Answers

A793

neuter

A794

aquel

A795

ESTO

Questions

Q796

(THAT) edificio a lo lejos es muy moderno.

*Your Own Answer*_____

Q797

(THESE) problemas son difíciles de resolver.

*Your Own Answer*_____

Q798

Jaime e Isabel son novios, (THE FORMER) va a volver de España pronto.

*Your Own Answer*_____

Correct Answers

A796

AQUEL

A797

ESTOS

A798

AQUÉL

Questions

Q799

En (THAT) época los reyes católicos reinaron en España.

*Your Own Answer*_____

Q800

Me gustan (THOSE) guantes de algodón.

*Your Own Answer*_____

Q801

Esos calcetines y (THESE) cuestan demasiado.

*Your Own Answer*_____

Correct Answers

A799

AQUELLA

A800

ESOS

A801

ÉSTOS

Questions

Q802

Nunca paga nada y (THAT) me da rabia.

Your Own Answer_____

Q803

Muéstreme otro vestido, no me gusta (THIS ONE).

Your Own Answer_____

Q804

Siempre llega tarde y (THAT) me da rabia.

Your Own Answer_____

Correct Answers

A802

ESO

A803

ÉSTE

A804

ESO

Questions

Q805

(THESE) problemas son fáciles de resolver.

Your Own Answer_____

Q806

Mi corbata y _____ Juan son de cuero.

Your Own Answer_____

Q807

Los dos decidieron casarse (BY) julio.

Your Own Answer_____

Correct Answers

A805

ESTOS

A806

la de

A807

PARA

Questions

Q808

Ha sido gobernader (FOR) tres años.

Your Own Answer

Q809

Mis padres trabajan (FOR) una compañía pequeña.

Your Own Answer

Q810

Vamos al parque (THROUGH) el parque.

Your Own Answer

Correct Answers

A808

POR

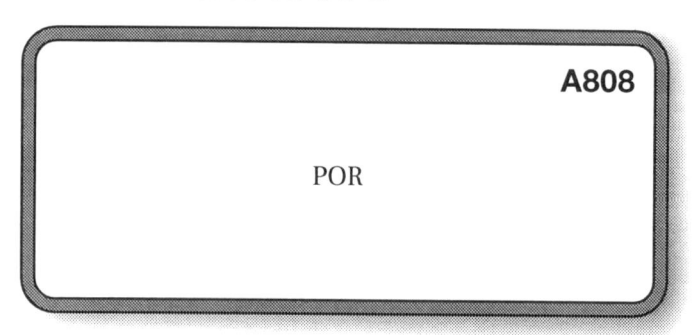

A809

PARA

A810

POR

Questions

Q811

Necesitas aprender esta información (BY) el viernes.

*Your Own Answer*___

Q812

¿Cuánto pageste (FOR) ese abrigo de lana?

*Your Own Answer*___

Q813

(IN ORDER TO) ir al centro tienes que pasar (THROUGH) esa calle.

*Your Own Answer*___

Correct Answers

A811

PARA

A812

POR

A813

PARA; POR

Questions

Q814

Fumar no es bueno (FOR) la salud.

*Your Own Answer*_____

Q815

Fue construida (BY) un arquitecto famoso.

*Your Own Answer*_____

Q816

Debemos luchar (FOR) nuestros derechos.

*Your Own Answer*_____

Correct Answers

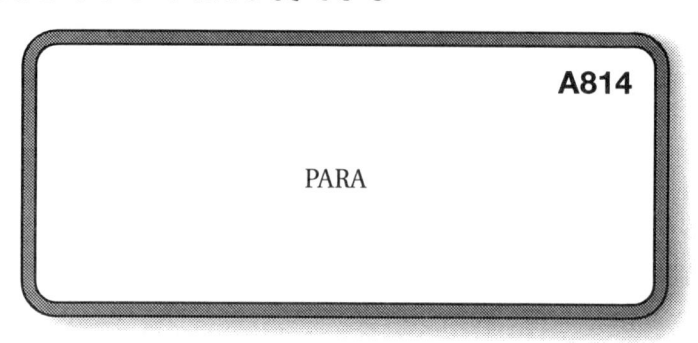

A814

PARA

A815

POR

A816

POR

Questions

Q817

Lo hice todo (FOR) ti.

*Your Own Answer*_____

Q818

(FOR) niño, se comporta muy bien.

*Your Own Answer*_____

Q819

Ganaba cien dólares (PER) semana.

*Your Own Answer*_____

Correct Answers

A817

POR

A818

PARA

A819

POR

Questions

Q820

¿Cuánto dinero me pagarás (FOR) mi trabajo?

*Your Own Answer*_____

Q821

Esos atletas son más altos (THAN) puedes creer.

*Your Own Answer*_____

Q822

Siempre compra más ropa (THAN) puede llevar.

*Your Own Answer*_____

Correct Answers

A820

POR

A821

DE LO QUE

A822

DE LA QUE

Questions

Q823

In an unequal comparison _____ will precede the noun, adjective or adverb, and _____ will follow.

*Your Own Answer*_____

Q824

Juanita es más guapa (THAN) Isabel.

*Your Own Answer*_____

Q825

Ellos tienen más libros (THAN) pueden contar.

*Your Own Answer*_____

Correct Answers

A823

más, que

A824

QUE

A825

DE LOS QUE

Questions

Q826

Esta información es más importante (THAN) tú puedes imaginarte.

*Your Own Answer*_____

Q827

Yo soy (AS) alta (AS) mi hermana menor.

*Your Own Answer*_____

Q828

Había (AS MANY) flores (AS) árboles en el jardín.

*Your Own Answer*_____

Correct Answers

A826

DE LO QUE

A827

TAN; COMO

A828

TANTAS; COMO

Questions

Q829

Esas chicas son (THE MOST) simpáticas.

*Your Own Answer*_____

Q830

Raúl y Anita son (THE MOST) inteligentes de la clase.

*Your Own Answer*_____

Q831

To express "on" with a day of the week in Spanish, the _____ is used.

*Your Own Answer*_____

Correct Answers

A829

LAS MÁS

A830

LOS MÁS

A831

definite article

Questions

Q832

In Spanish, to express the time of day one must use _____ or _____ before the hour.

Your Own Answer_____

Q833

Two possible translations for *lo importante* are _____.

Your Own Answer_____

Q834

A large number of words ending in -ma, -pa, or -ta (i.e. *idioma, mapa, profeta*) are _____ in gender.

Your Own Answer_____

Correct Answers

A832

la; las

A833

the important part or thing

A834

masculine

Questions

Q835

(THE) programa no vale la pena.

*Your Own Answer*_____

Q836

(THE BEST THING) es estudiar cada día.

*Your Own Answer*_____

Q837

What is the corresponding future tense for *quepo* (I fit)?

*Your Own Answer*_____

Correct Answers

A835

EL

A836

LO MEJOR

A837

cabré

Questions

Q838

What is the corresponding future tense for *puedes* (you can)?

*Your Own Answer*_____

Q839

What is the corresponding future tense for *queremos* (we want)?

*Your Own Answer*_____

Q840

What is the corresponding future tense for *saben* (they know)?

*Your Own Answer*_____

Correct Answers

A838

podrás

A839

querremos

A840

sabrán

Questions

Q841

What is the corresponding future tense for *ponéis* (you put)?

*Your Own Answer*_____

Q842

What is the corresponding future tense for *vale* (it is worth)?

*Your Own Answer*_____

Q843

What is the corresponding future tense for *vienes* (you come)?

*Your Own Answer*_____

Correct Answers

A841

pondréis

A842

valdrá

A843

vendrás

Questions

Q844

What is the corresponding future tense for *digo* (I say)?

*Your Own Answer*_____

Q845

What is the corresponding future tense for *hacen* (they make/do)?

*Your Own Answer*_____

Q846

What is the corresponding future tense for *tenemos* (we have)?

*Your Own Answer*_____

Correct Answers

A844

diré

A845

harán

A846

tendremos

Questions

Q847

What is the corresponding future tense for *salís* (you leave)?

Your Own Answer_____

Q848

What is the corresponding future tense for *he* (I have-aux)?

Your Own Answer_____

Q849

What is the corresponding conditional tense for *quepo* (I fit)?

Your Own Answer_____

Correct Answers

A847

saldréis

A848

habré

A849

cabría

Questions

Q850

What is the corresponding conditional tense for *puedes* (you can)?

*Your Own Answer*_____

Q851

What is the corresponding conditional tense for *queremos* (we want)?

*Your Own Answer*_____

Q852

What is the corresponding conditional tense for *saben* (they know)?

*Your Own Answer*_____

Correct Answers

A850

podrías

A851

querríamos

A852

sabrían

Questions

Q853

What is the corresponding conditional tense for *ponéis* (you put)?

Your Own Answer_____

Q854

What is the corresponding conditional tense for *vale* (it is worth)?

Your Own Answer_____

Q855

What is the corresponding conditional tense for *vienes* (you come)?

Your Own Answer_____

Correct Answers

A853

pondríais

A854

valdría

A855

vendrías

Questions

Q856

What is the corresponding conditional tense for *digo* (I say)?

Your Own Answer_____

Q857

What is the corresponding conditional tense for *hacen* (they make/do)?

Your Own Answer_____

Q858

What is the corresponding conditional tense for *tenemos* (we have)?

Your Own Answer_____

Correct Answers

A856

diría

A857

harían

A858

tendríamos

Questions

Q859

What is the corresponding conditional tense for *salís* (you leave)?

*Your Own Answer*_____

Q860

What is the corresponding conditional tense for *he* (I have-aux)?

*Your Own Answer*_____

Q861

In addition to meaning "will" or "shall" the future tense in Spanish is also used to express _____ probability.

*Your Own Answer*_____

Correct Answers

A859

saldríais

A860

habría

A861

present

Questions

Q862

In addition to meaning "would", the conditional tense in Spanish is also used to express _____ probability.

*Your Own Answer*_____

Q863

When "would" may be translated as "used to" in Spanish instead of the conditional tense, the _____ is used.

*Your Own Answer*_____

Q864

The verbs *acabar de* (to have just) and *solar* (to be accustomed to) are defective and are commonly used in two tenses only, the _____ and the _____.

*Your Own Answer*_____

Correct Answers

A862

past

A863

imperfect

A864

present; imperfect

Questions

Q865

¿Qué hora era cuando llegó? IT MUST HAVE BEEN (SER) las doce.

*Your Own Answer*_____

Q866

Todavía no ha llegado. ¿Dónde CAN HE BE (ESTAR)?

*Your Own Answer*_____

Q867

Para mañana yo (TERMINAR) todo el trabajo.

*Your Own Answer*_____

Correct Answers

A865

SERÍAN

A866

ESTARÁ

A867

HABRÉ TERMINADO

Questions

Q868

Si Juan fuera rico, (COMPRAR) un Ferrari.

*Your Own Answer*_____

Q869

Ella (ACABAR) de entrar cuando se cayó.

*Your Own Answer*_____

Q870

What is the present participle for *volver* (returning)?

*Your Own Answer*_____

Correct Answers

A868

COMPRARÍA

A869

ACABABA

A870

VOLVIENDO

Questions

Q871

What is the present participle for *abrir* (opening)?

*Your Own Answer*_____

Q872

What is the present participle for *cubrir* (covering)?

*Your Own Answer*_____

Q873

What is the present participle for *romper* (breaking)?

*Your Own Answer*_____

Correct Answers

A871

abriendo

A872

cubriendo

A873

rompiendo

Questions

Q874

What is the present participle for *ir* (going)?

Your Own Answer_____

Q875

What is the present participle for *poder* (being able)?

Your Own Answer_____

Q876

What is the present participle for *venir* (coming)?

Your Own Answer_____

Correct Answers

A874

yendo

A875

pudiendo

A876

viniendo

Questions

Q877

What is the present participle for *decir* (saying)?

*Your Own Answer*_____

Q878

What is the present participle for *escribir* (writing)?

*Your Own Answer*_____

Q879

What is the present participle for *hacer* (doing/making)?

*Your Own Answer*_____

Correct Answers

A877

diciendo

A878

escribiendo

A879

haciendo

Questions

Q880

What is the present participle for *ver* (seeing)?

*Your Own Answer*_____

Q881

What is the present participle for *poner* (putting)?

*Your Own Answer*_____

Q882

What is the present participle for *morir* (dying)?

*Your Own Answer*_____

Correct Answers

A880

viendo

A881

poniendo

A882

muriendo

Questions

Q883

What is the present participle for *caer* (falling)?

*Your Own Answer*_____

Q884

What is the past participle for *volver* (returned)?

*Your Own Answer*_____

Q885

What is the past participle for *abrir* (opened)?

*Your Own Answer*_____

Correct Answers

A883

cayendo

A884

vuelto

A885

abierto

Questions

Q886

What is the past participle for *cubrir* (covered)?

Your Own Answer

Q887

What is the past participle for *romper* (broken)?

Your Own Answer

Q888

What is the past participle for *ir* (gone)?

Your Own Answer

Correct Answers

A886

cubierto

A887

roto

A888

ido

Questions

Q889

What is the past participle for *poder* (been able)?

*Your Own Answer*_____

Q890

What is the past participle for *venir* (came)?

*Your Own Answer*_____

Q891

What is the past participle for *decir* (said)?

*Your Own Answer*_____

Correct Answers

A889

podido

A890

venido

A891

dicho

Questions

Q892

What is the past participle for *escribir* (written)?

Your Own Answer_____

Q893

What is the past participle for *hacer* (done/made)?

Your Own Answer_____

Q894

What is the past participle for *ver* (seen)?

Your Own Answer_____

Correct Answers

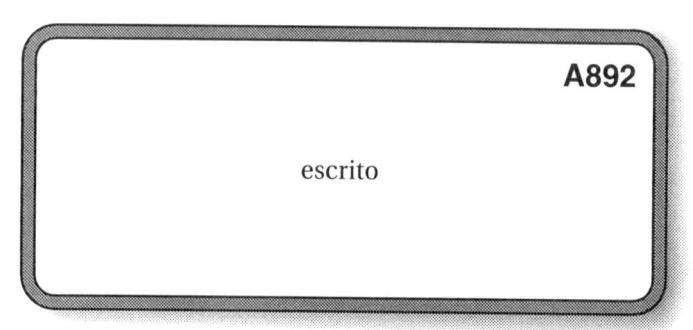

A892

escrito

A893

hecho

A894

visto

Questions

Q895

What is the past participle for *poner* (put)?

*Your Own Answer*_____

Q896

What is the past participle for *morir* (dead)?

*Your Own Answer*_____

Q897

What is the past participle for *caer* (fallen)?

*Your Own Answer*_____

Correct Answers

A895

puesto

A896

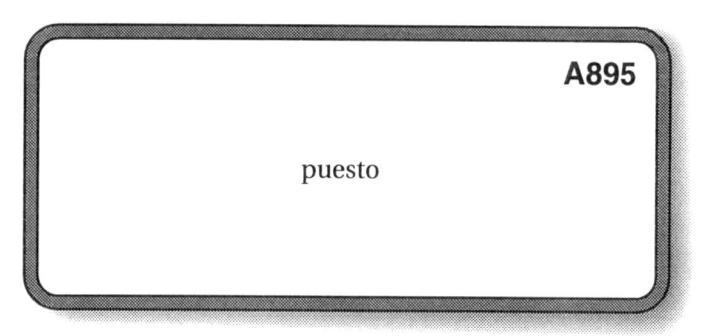

muerto

A897

caído

Questions

Q898

The past participle (-ed) in Spanish is commonly used with the helping verb _____.

Your Own Answer _____

Q899

The present participle (-ing) in Spanish is commonly used with the helping verb _____.

Your Own Answer _____

Q900

The past participle in Spanish may also function as an _____.

Your Own Answer _____

Correct Answers

A898

haber

A899

estar

A900

adjective

Questions

Q901

Verb forms which follow forms of *seguir* (to keep on) and *continuar* (to continue) must be _____.

*Your Own Answer*_____

Q902

Object pronouns used with the present participle must be placed _____.

*Your Own Answer*_____

Q903

(HAVING HEARD) al testigo, decidió condenar al prisionero.

*Your Own Answer*_____

Correct Answers

A901

present participles

A902

after + attached

A903

HABIENDO OÍDO

Questions

Q904

La madre de mi esposa es mi _____.

*Your Own Answer*_____

Q905

Llamamos a una persona que no quiere trabajar _____.

*Your Own Answer*_____

Q906

(THE BEES) vuelan de flor en flor.

*Your Own Answer*_____

Correct Answers

A904

suegra

A905

floja/perezosa

A906

LAS ABEJAS

Questions

Q907

El dinero que recibo cada semana por mi trabajo es mi _____.

*Your Own Answer*_____

Q908

Los insectos usan _____ para volar.

*Your Own Answer*_____

Q909

Una persona que requiere una peluca es _____.

*Your Own Answer*_____

Correct Answers

A907

sueldo

A908

las alas

A909

calva

Questions

Q910

Al cortarme la mano el médico me puso una (BANDAGE).

Your Own Answer_____

Q911

Le dio a su novia un ramillete de (FLOWERS).

Your Own Answer_____

Q912

Usamos una aguja e hilo para (TO SEW).

Your Own Answer_____

Correct Answers

A910

VENDA

A911

FLORES

A912

COSER

Questions

Q913

Para ir de merienda voy al (COUNTRYSIDE).

*Your Own Answer*_____

Q914

Un albañil ayuda a construir (BUILDINGS).

*Your Own Answer*_____

Q915

Espero el tren en el (PLATFORM).

*Your Own Answer*_____

Correct Answers

A913

CAMPO

A914

EDIFICIOS

A915

ANDÉN

Questions

Q916

Debemos (TO PLANT) una semilla.

*Your Own Answer*_____

Q917

El opuesto de SALVAJE es _____.

*Your Own Answer*_____

Q918

Una azafata trabaja en (A PLANE).

*Your Own Answer*_____

Correct Answers

A916

PLANTAR

A917

MANSO

A918

UN AVIÓN

Questions

Q919

El opuesto de AMARGO es _____.

*Your Own Answer*_____

Q920

Una persona DESCALZA necesita (SHOES).

*Your Own Answer*_____

Q921

Se asocia EL TRUENO con (THE RAIN).

*Your Own Answer*_____

Correct Answers

A919

DULCE

A920

ZAPATOS

A921

LA LLUVIA

Questions

Q922

Se pone una sortija en (THE FINGER).

*Your Own Answer*_____

Q923

El opuesto de APRESURAR (SE) es _____.

*Your Own Answer*_____

Q924

El sinónimo de LUGAR es _____.

*Your Own Answer*_____

Correct Answers

A922

EL DEDO

A923

TARDAR(SE)

A924

SITIO

Questions

Q925

El opuesto de macho es _____.

*Your Own Answer*_____

Q926

Al morir su esposo la mujer quedó (WIDOW).

*Your Own Answer*_____

Q927

El alumno sólo puede escribir con la mano izquierda porque es _____.

*Your Own Answer*_____

Correct Answers

A925

hembra

A926

VIUDA

A927

zurdo

Questions

Q928

Si el grifo está goteando hay que _____ la llave.

*Your Own Answer*_____

Q929

Si uno sufre de una tos grave tiene (A COLD).

*Your Own Answer*_____

Q930

Por haber sobrepasado la velocidad tuve que pagar una _____.

*Your Own Answer*_____

Correct Answers

A928

cerrar

A929

UN CATARRO

A930

multa

Questions

Q931

Para comprar entradas para el concierto, fui a la (BOX OFFICE).

*Your Own Answer*_____

Q932

En un rebaño se hallan (SHEEP).

*Your Own Answer*_____

Q933

El ladrón acabó _____ admitir el crimen.

*Your Own Answer*_____

Correct Answers

A931

TAQUILLA

A932

OVEJAS

A933

por

Questions

Q934

Si "hago pedazos" el papel, lo _____.

*Your Own Answer*_____

Q935

Hay demasiadas arrugas en la camisa. Tengo que _____.

*Your Own Answer*_____

Q936

La niña quedó sin padres; o sea, es _____.

*Your Own Answer*_____

Correct Answers

A934

rompo

A935

plancharla

A936

huérfana

Questions

Q937

Juana era tuerta; es decir, le faltaba _____.

*Your Own Answer*_____

Q938

Para evitar ir a la cárcel, el hombre tuvo que pagar (A FINE).

*Your Own Answer*_____

Q939

Roberto es sordo; es decir, no puede _____.

*Your Own Answer*_____

Correct Answers

A937

un ojo

A938

UNA MULTA

A939

oír

Questions

Q940

Una persona muda no puede _____.

*Your Own Answer*_____

Q941

Una vez más Juan (MISSED) el tren por haber llegado tarde.

*Your Own Answer*_____

Q942

(THERE WERE) varios accidentes en esa calle.

*Your Own Answer*_____

Correct Answers

A940

hablar

A941

PERDIÓ

A942

HUBO/HABÍA

Questions

Q943

Tengo que llegar pronto; tengo (HASTE).

*Your Own Answer*_____

Q944

Ella (WENT CRAZY) al oír las malas noticias.

*Your Own Answer*_____

Q945

El soldado luchó por su (HOMELAND).

*Your Own Answer*_____

Correct Answers

A943

PRISA

A944

SE VOLVIÓ LOCA

A945

PATRIA

Questions

Q946

Conocí a Berta por primera vez cuando Roberto me la (INTRODUCED).

*Your Own Answer*_____

Q947

What is the present subjunctive for *espere* (wait for)?

*Your Own Answer*_____

Q948

What is the present subjunctive for *decida* (decide)?

*Your Own Answer*_____

Correct Answers

A946

PRESENTÓ

A947

esperara

A948

decidiera

Questions

Q949

What is the present subjunctive for *prefiera*?

*Your Own Answer*_____

Q950

What is the present subjunctive for *ponga*?

*Your Own Answer*_____

Q951

What is the present subjunctive for *lea*?

*Your Own Answer*_____

Correct Answers

A949

prefiriera

A950

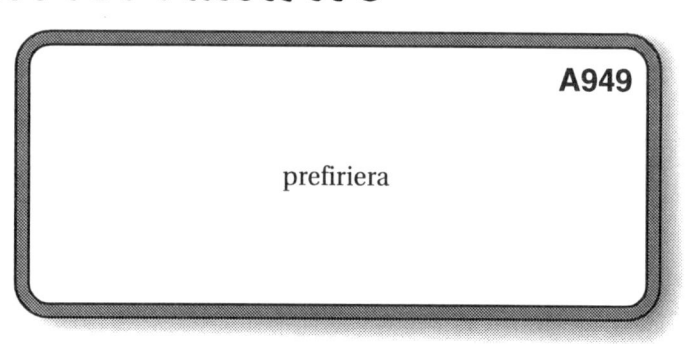

pusiera

A951

leyera

Questions

Q952

What is the present subjunctive for *entienda*?

*Your Own Answer*_____

Q953

What is the present subjunctive for *pregunte*?

*Your Own Answer*_____

Q954

What is the past subjunctive for *espere.*?

*Your Own Answer*_____

Correct Answers

A952

entendiera

A953

preguntara

A954

esperase

Questions

Q955

What is the past subjunctive for *decida*?

Your Own Answer_____

Q956

What is the past subjunctive for *prefiera*?

Your Own Answer_____

Q957

What is the past subjunctive for *ponga*?

Your Own Answer_____

Correct Answers

A955

decidiese

A956

prefiriese

A957

pusiese

Questions

Q958

What is the past subjunctive for *lea*?

*Your Own Answer*_____

Q959

What is the past subjunctive for *entienda*?

*Your Own Answer*_____

Q960

What is the past subjunctive for *pregunte*?

*Your Own Answer*_____

Correct Answers

A958

leyese

A959

entendiese

A960

preguntase

Questions

Q961

Busco a alguien que (QUERER) compartir piso.

*Your Own Answer*_____

Q962

Te digo que (RECOGER) tus cosas ahora mismo.

*Your Own Answer*_____

Q963

Es verdad que él (VIVIR) con sus abuelos.

*Your Own Answer*_____

Correct Answers

A961

QUIERA

A962

RECOJAS

A963

VIVE

Questions

Q964

Cuando (VER) a Marta, dile que me llame.

*Your Own Answer*_____

Q965

Es imposible que (SER) ya tan mayor.

*Your Own Answer*_____

Q966

(IT'S) ya la una de la mañana.

*Your Own Answer*_____

Correct Answers

A964

VEAS

A965

SEA

A966

ES

Questions

Q967

No trabajan; (ARE) estudiantes.

*Your Own Answer*_____

Q968

Tus padres (ARE) comiendo en la cocina.

*Your Own Answer*_____

Q969

La mesa (IS) de madera de pino.

*Your Own Answer*_____

Correct Answers

A967

SON

A968

ESTÁN

A969

ES

Questions

Q970

El mes que viene tú (WILL BE) de vacaciones.

*Your Own Answer*_____

Q971

¿Dónde están (MY) cuadernos?

*Your Own Answer*_____

Q972

Tu corbata está aquí. ¿Y (YOUR) calcetines?

*Your Own Answer*_____

Correct Answers

A970

ESTARÁS

A971

MIS

A972

TUS

Questions

Q973

No me interesan (HER) cuadros.

*Your Own Answer*_____

Q974

Si esto sale mal, la culpa será (OURS).

*Your Own Answer*_____

Q975

Estas cajas no son mías; son (THEIRS).

*Your Own Answer*_____

Correct Answers

A973

SUS

A974

NUESTRA

A975

SUYAS

Questions

Q976

No sé qué es (THAT) que está allá arriba.

*Your Own Answer*_____

Q977

Este vaso es mío. ¿Es (THAT ONE) el tuyo?

*Your Own Answer*_____

Q978

Me gustan (THESE) camisas.

*Your Own Answer*_____

Correct Answers

A976

AQUELLO

A977

ÉSE

A978

ESTAS

Questions

Q979

¿Quién es (THAT) chica que está hablando con Pedro?

*Your Own Answer*_____

Q980

¿ _____ dónde se va para la estación?

*Your Own Answer*_____

Q981

Debes de caminar siempre _____ la acera.

*Your Own Answer*_____

Correct Answers

A979

AQUELLA

A980

Por

A981

por

Questions

Q982

No compré nada _____ mi tía.

*Your Own Answer*_____

Q983

Ha ido al bautizo _____ conocer a su nieta.

*Your Own Answer*_____

Q984

El hotel cobra cincuenta dólares _____ noche.

*Your Own Answer*_____

Correct Answers

A982

para

A983

para

A984

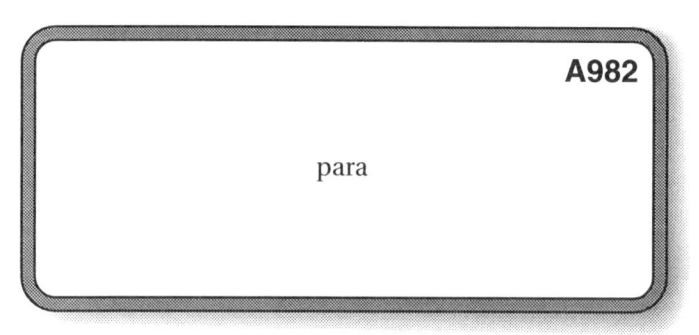

por

Questions

Q985

What is the present participle for *leer*?

*Your Own Answer*_____

Q986

What is the present participle for *traer*?

*Your Own Answer*_____

Q987

What is the present participle for *ser*?

*Your Own Answer*_____

Correct Answers

A985

leyendo (reading)

A986

trayendo (bringing)

A987

siendo (being)

Questions

Q988

What is the past participle for *leer*?

*Your Own Answer*_____

Q989

What is the past participle for *traer*?

*Your Own Answer*_____

Q990

What is the past participle for *ser*?

*Your Own Answer*_____

Correct Answers

A988

leído (read)

A989

traído (brought)

A990

sido (been)

BLANK CARDS
To Make Up Your Own Questions

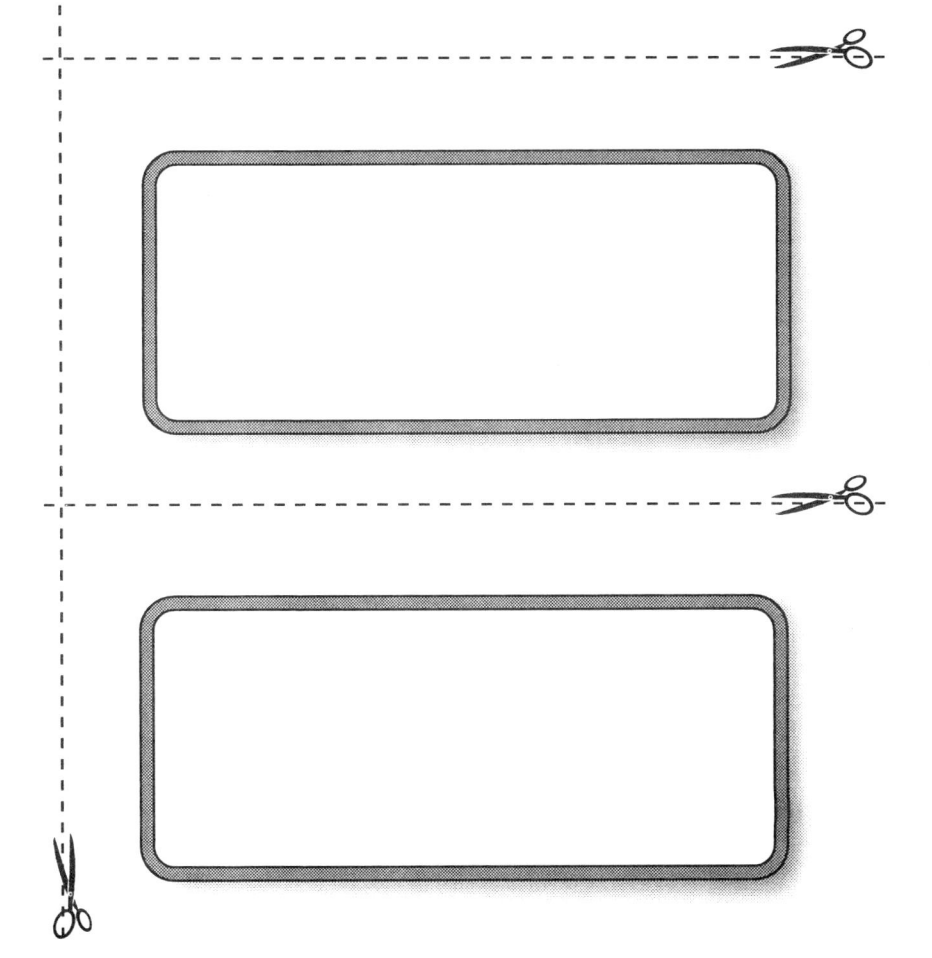

CORRECT ANSWERS
for
Your Own Questions

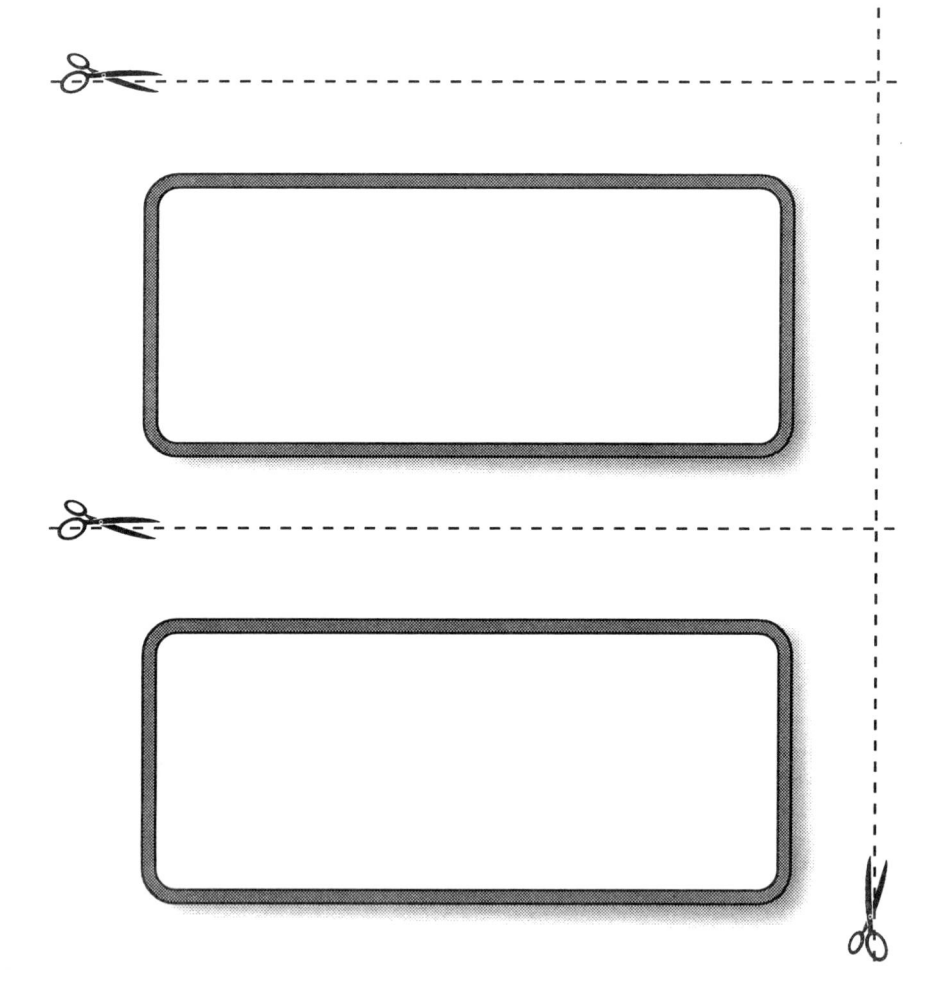

Blank Cards for *Your Own Questions*

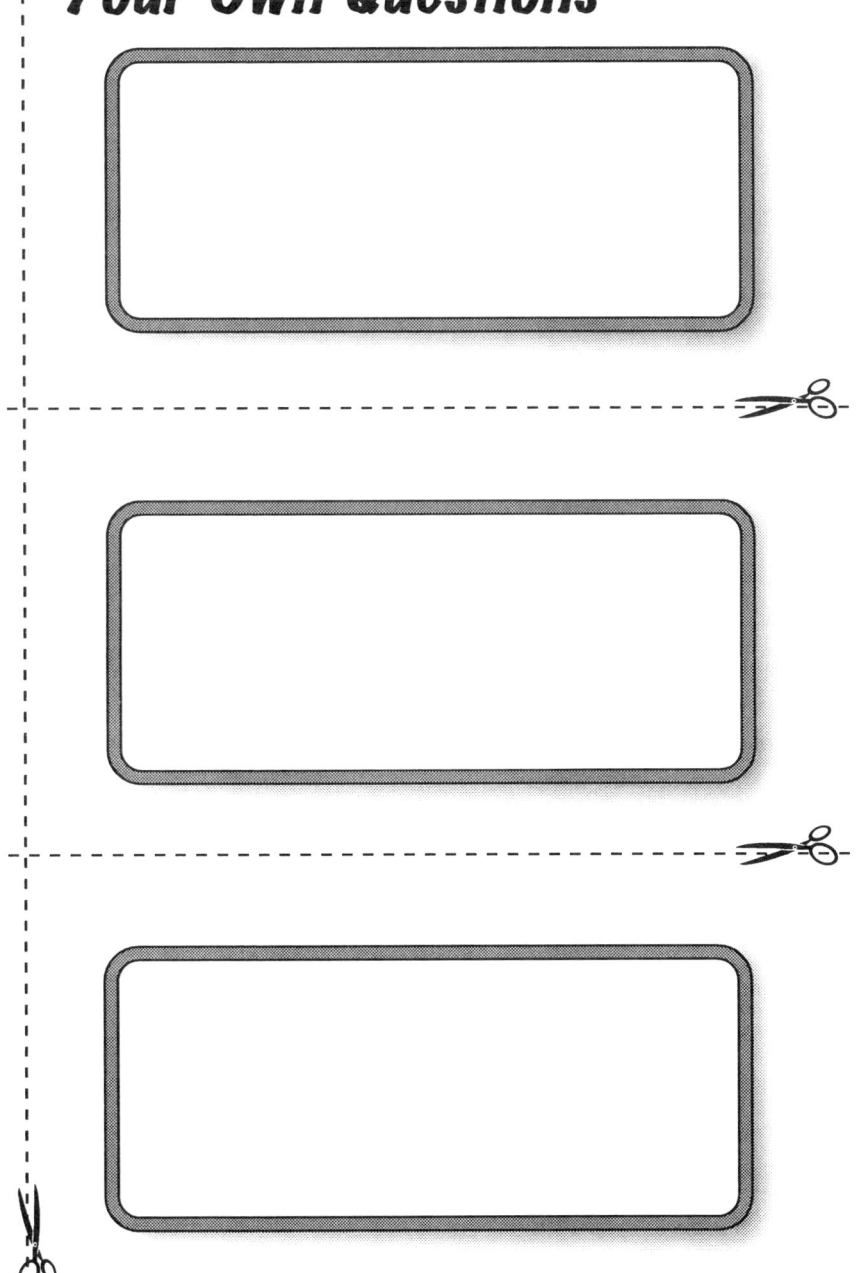

Correct Answers

Blank Cards for
Your Own Questions

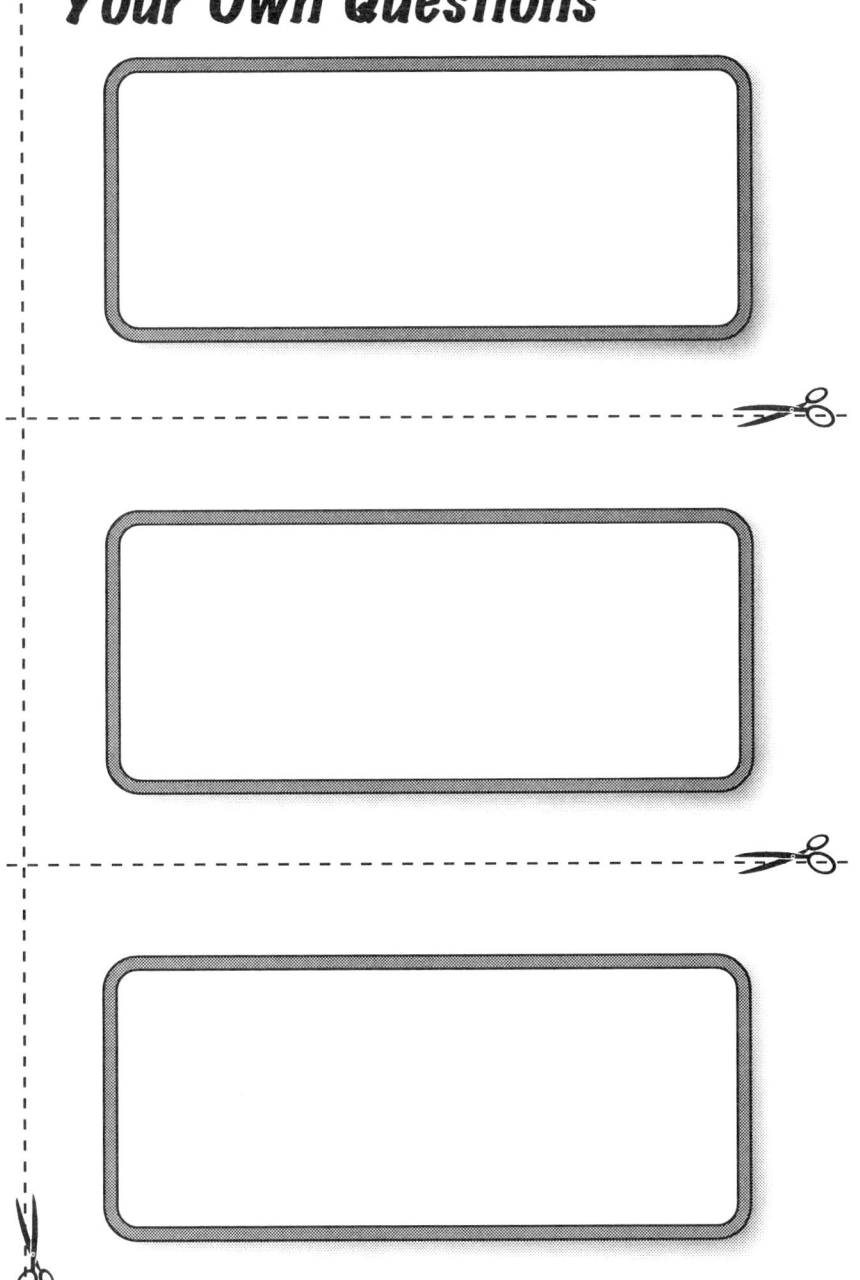

Correct Answers

Blank Cards for
Your Own Questions

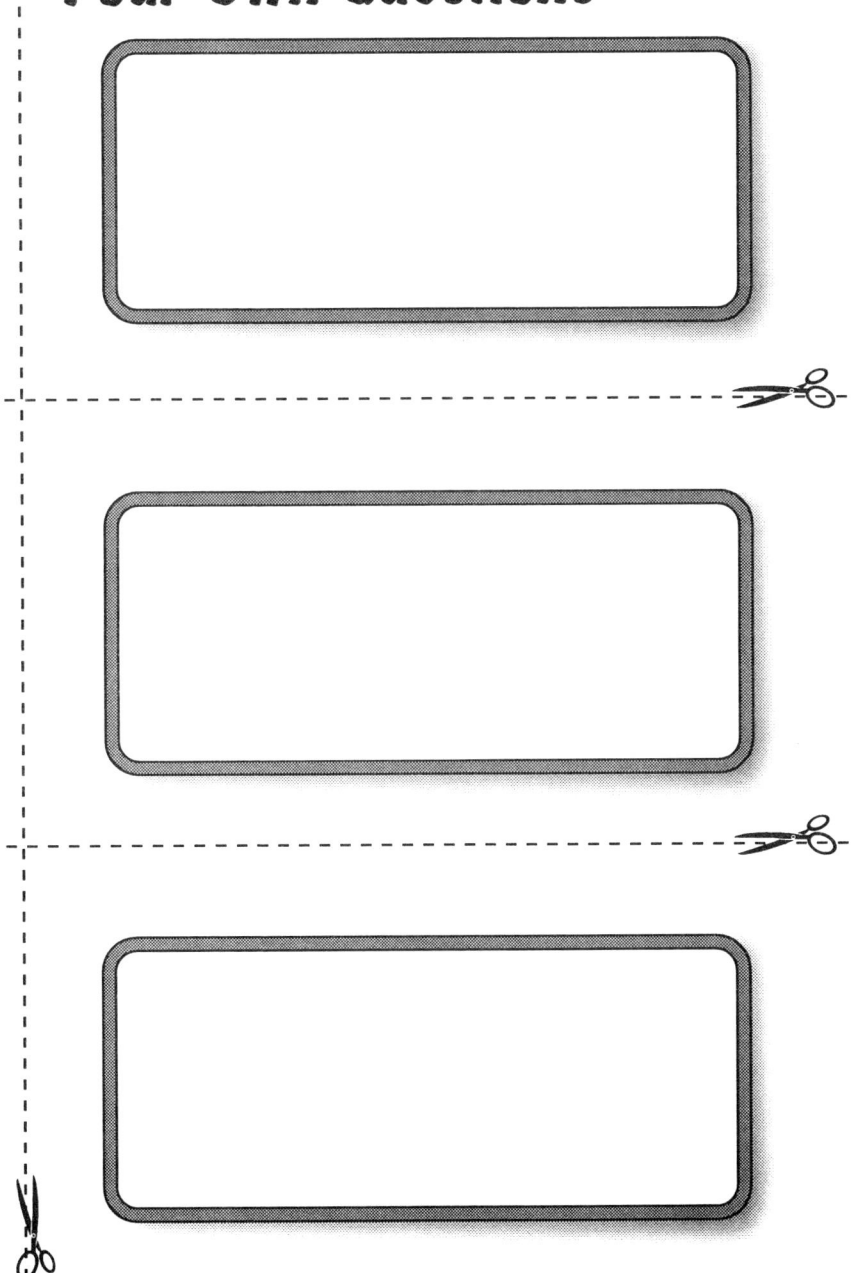

Correct Answers

Blank Cards for
Your Own Questions

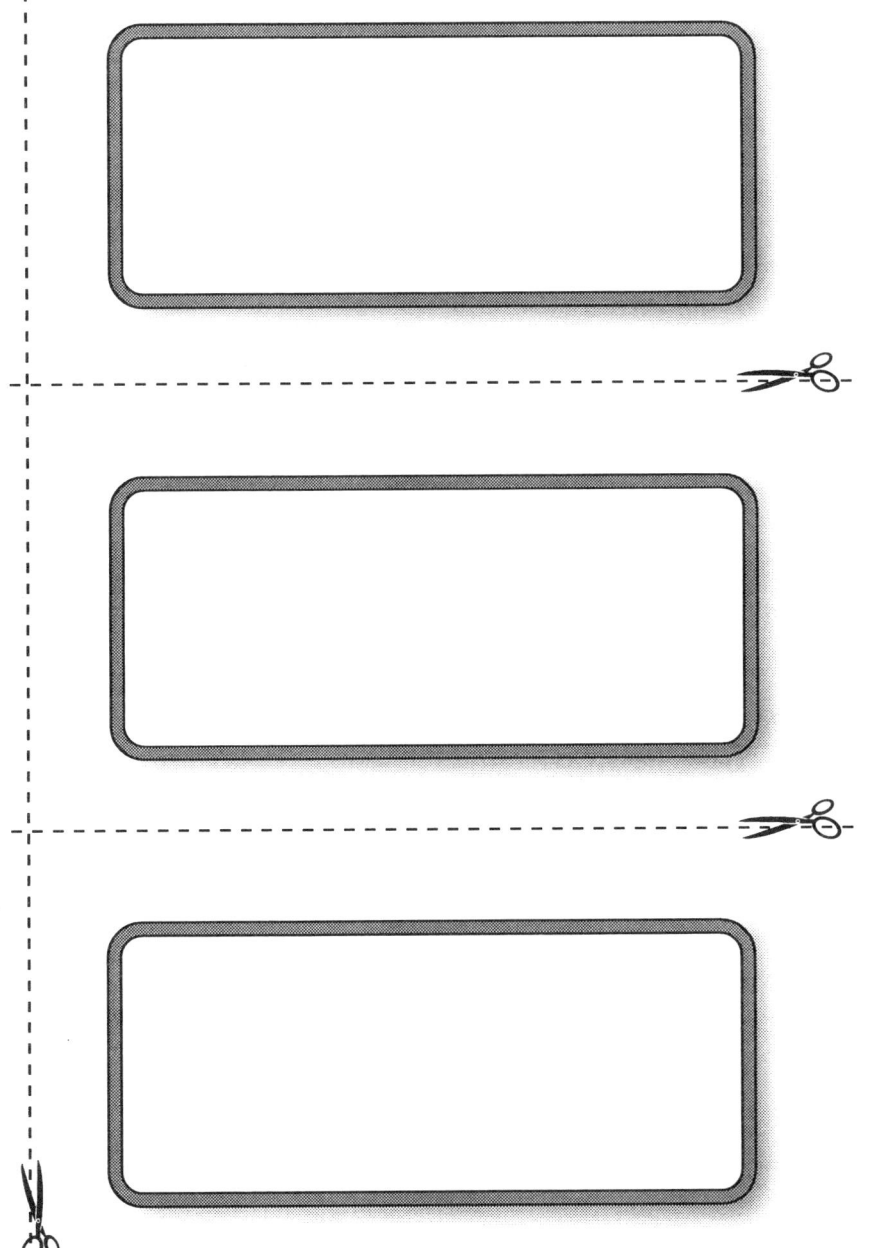

Correct Answers

Blank Cards for
Your Own Questions

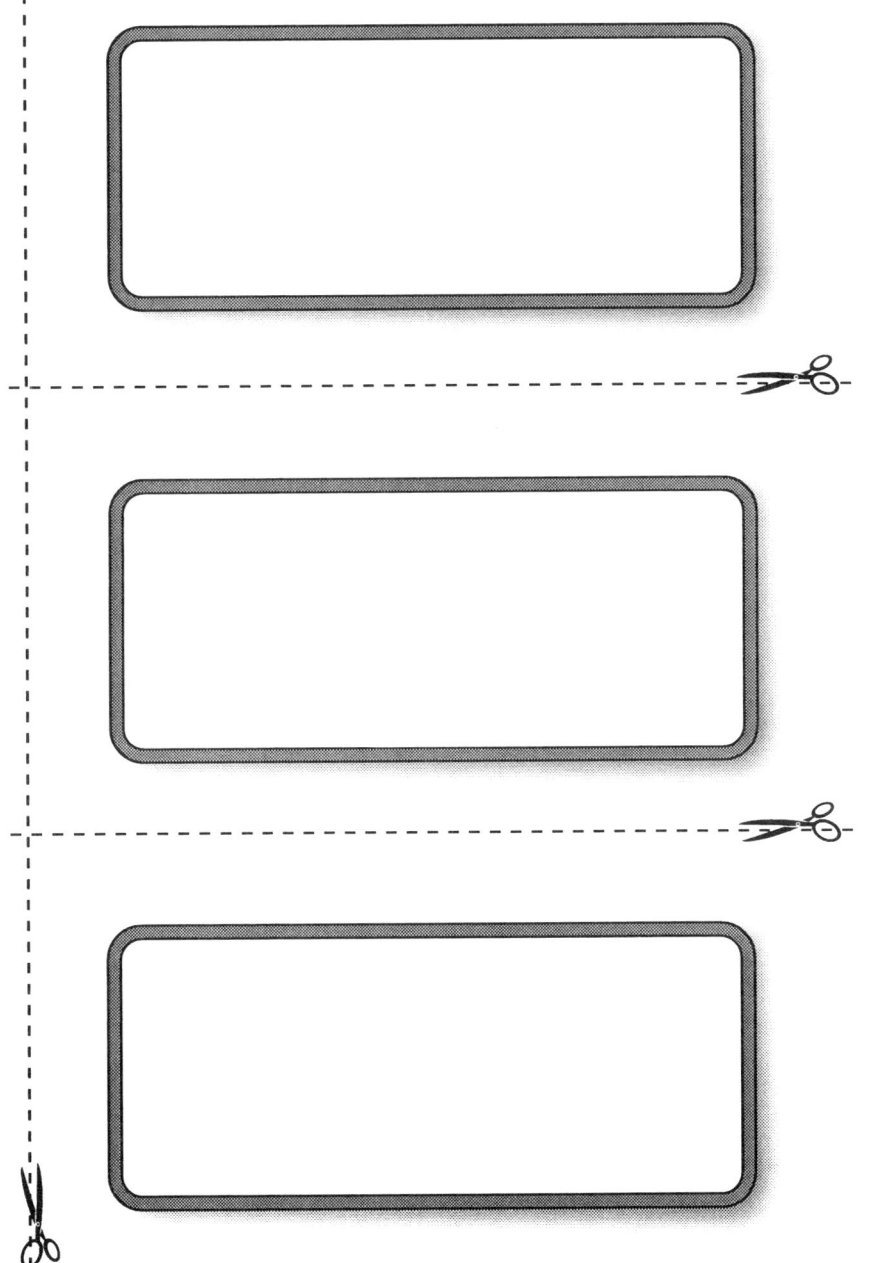

Correct Answers

Blank Cards for *Your Own Questions*

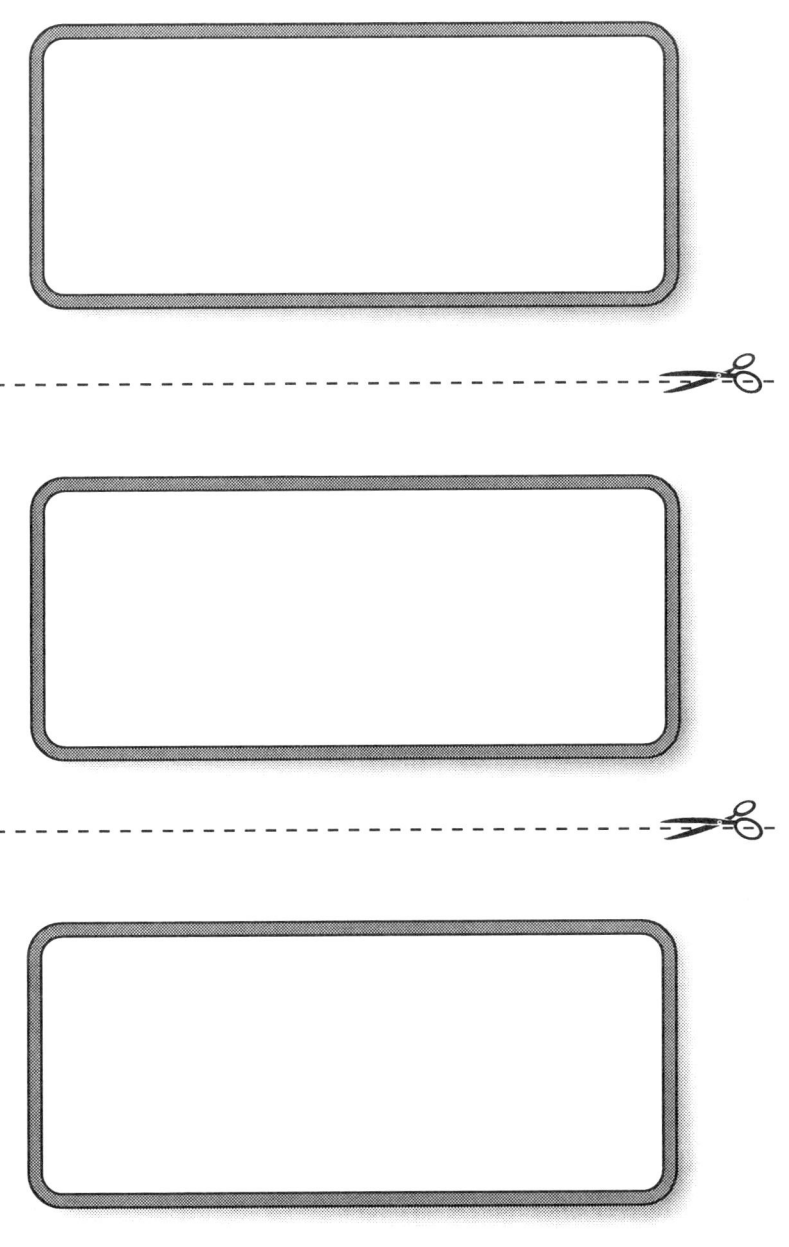

Correct Answers

Blank Cards for
Your Own Questions

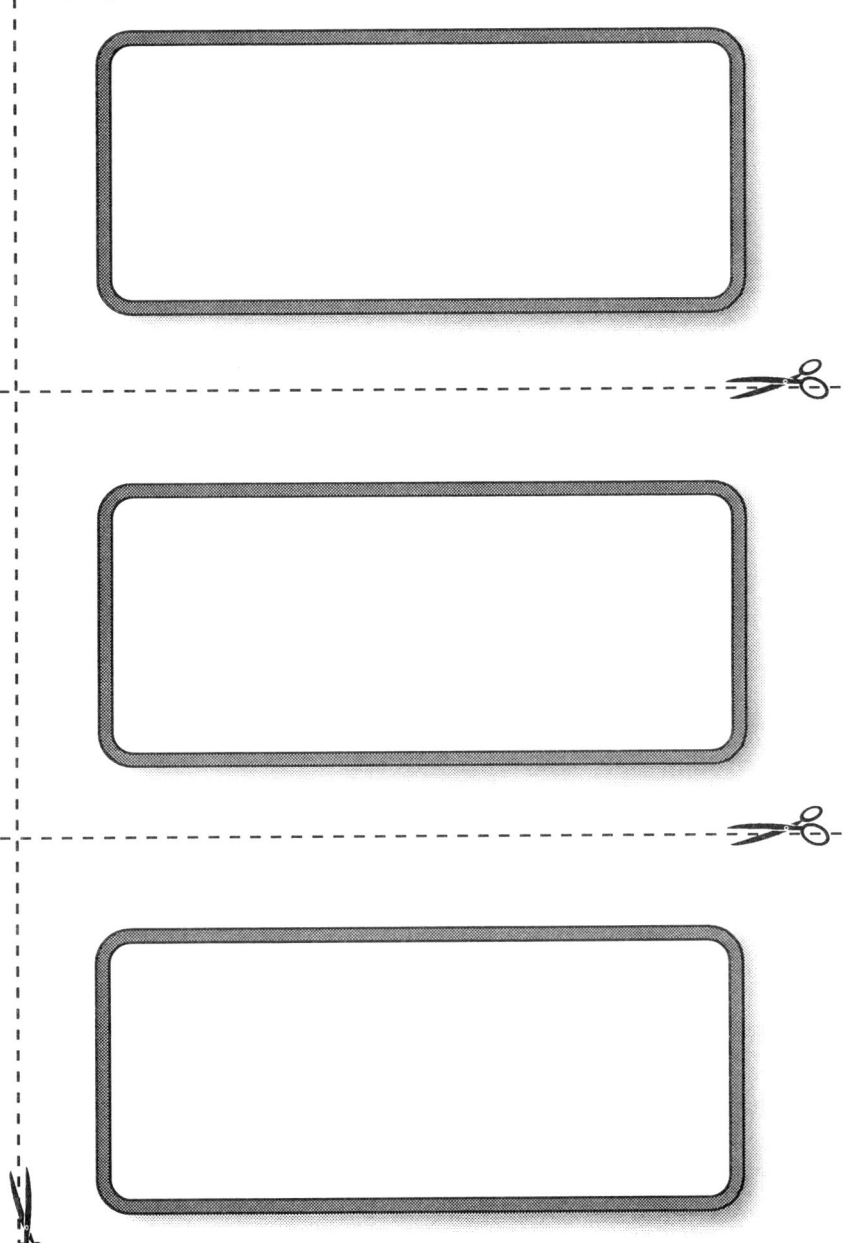

Correct Answers

Blank Cards for
Your Own Questions

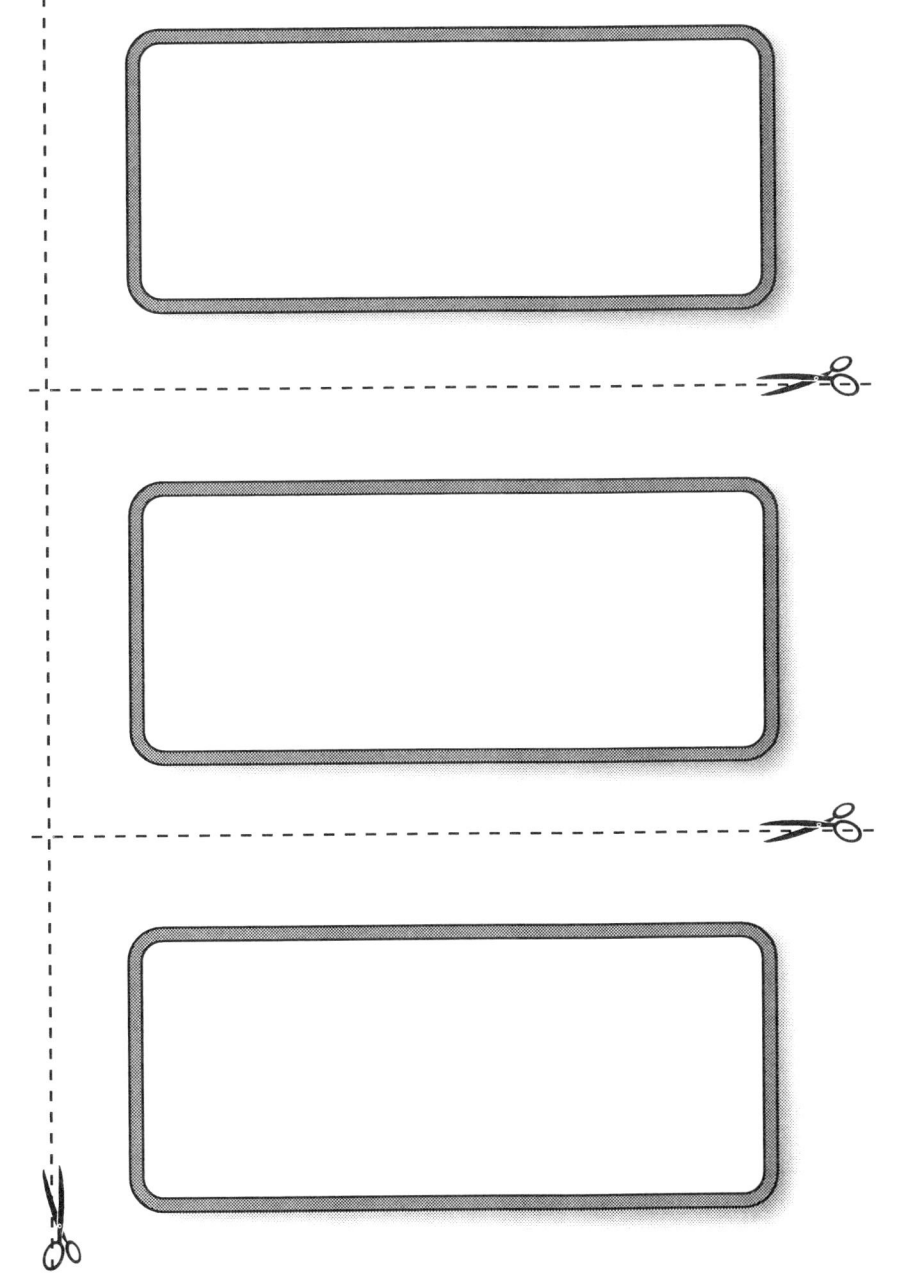

Correct Answers

Blank Cards for *Your Own Questions*

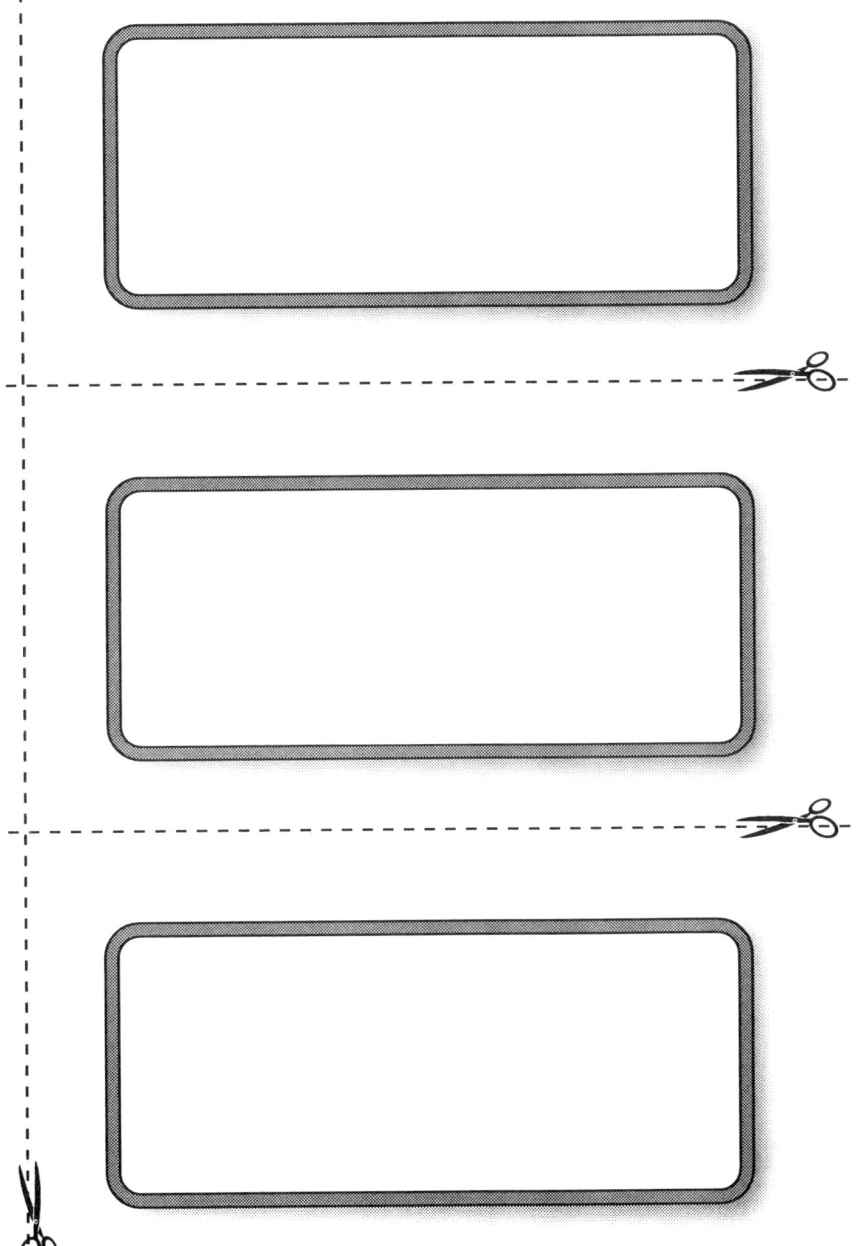

Correct Answers

Blank Cards for
Your Own Questions

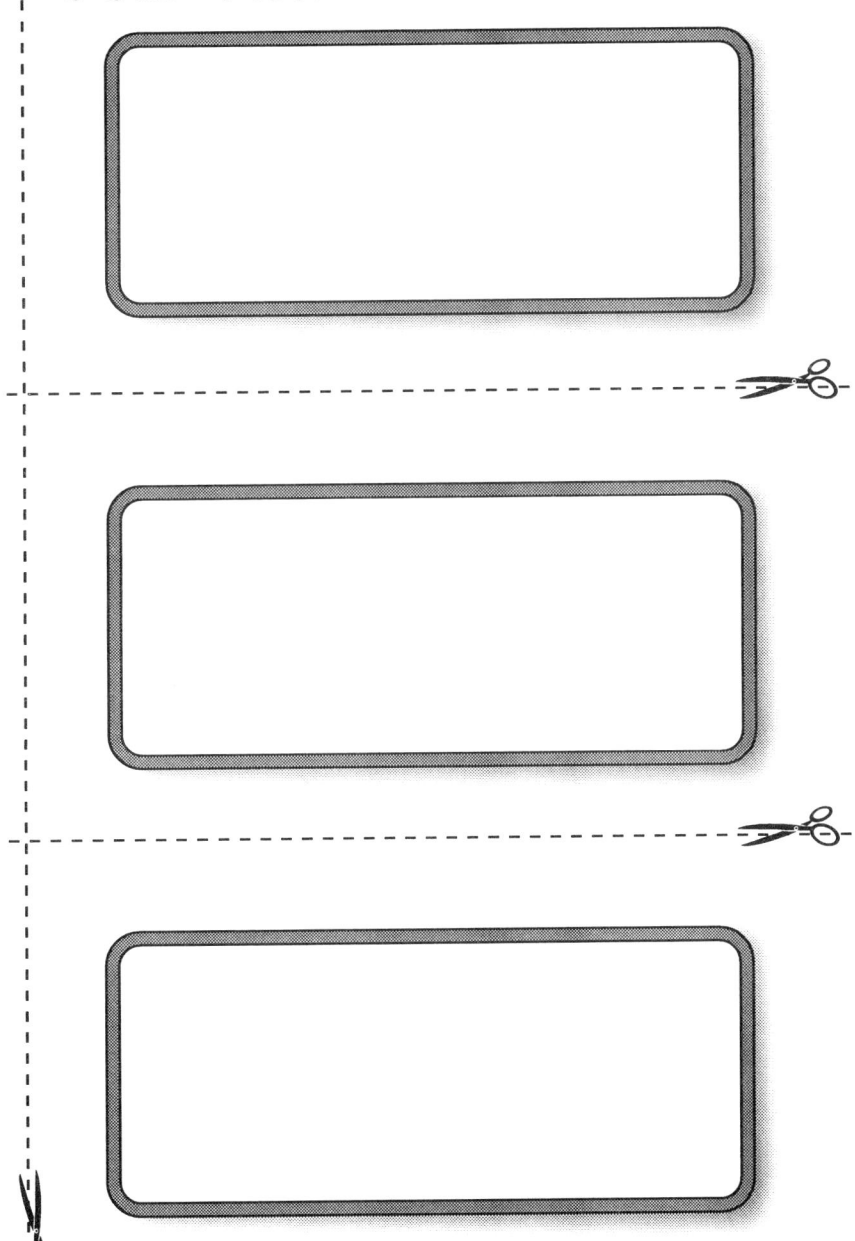

Correct Answers

Blank Cards for
Your Own Questions

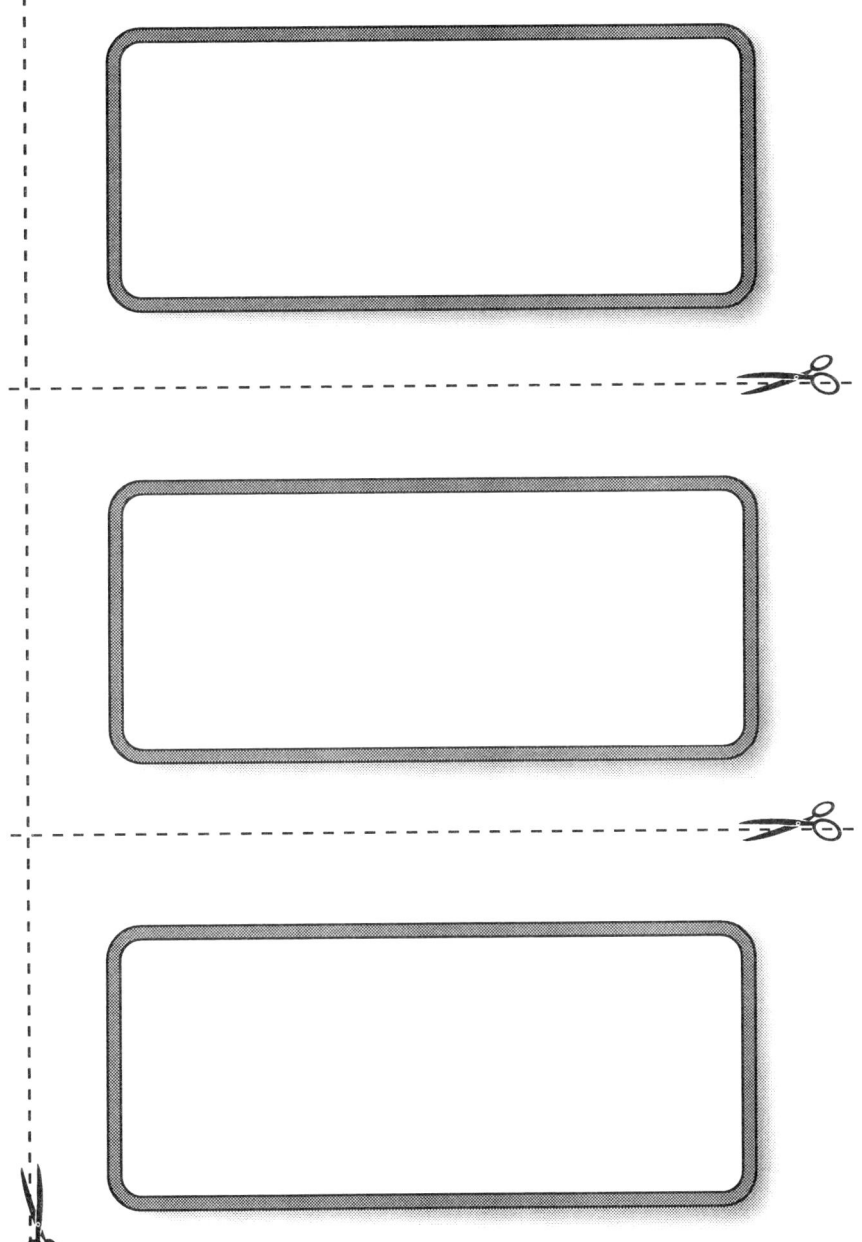

Correct Answers

Blank Cards for
Your Own Questions

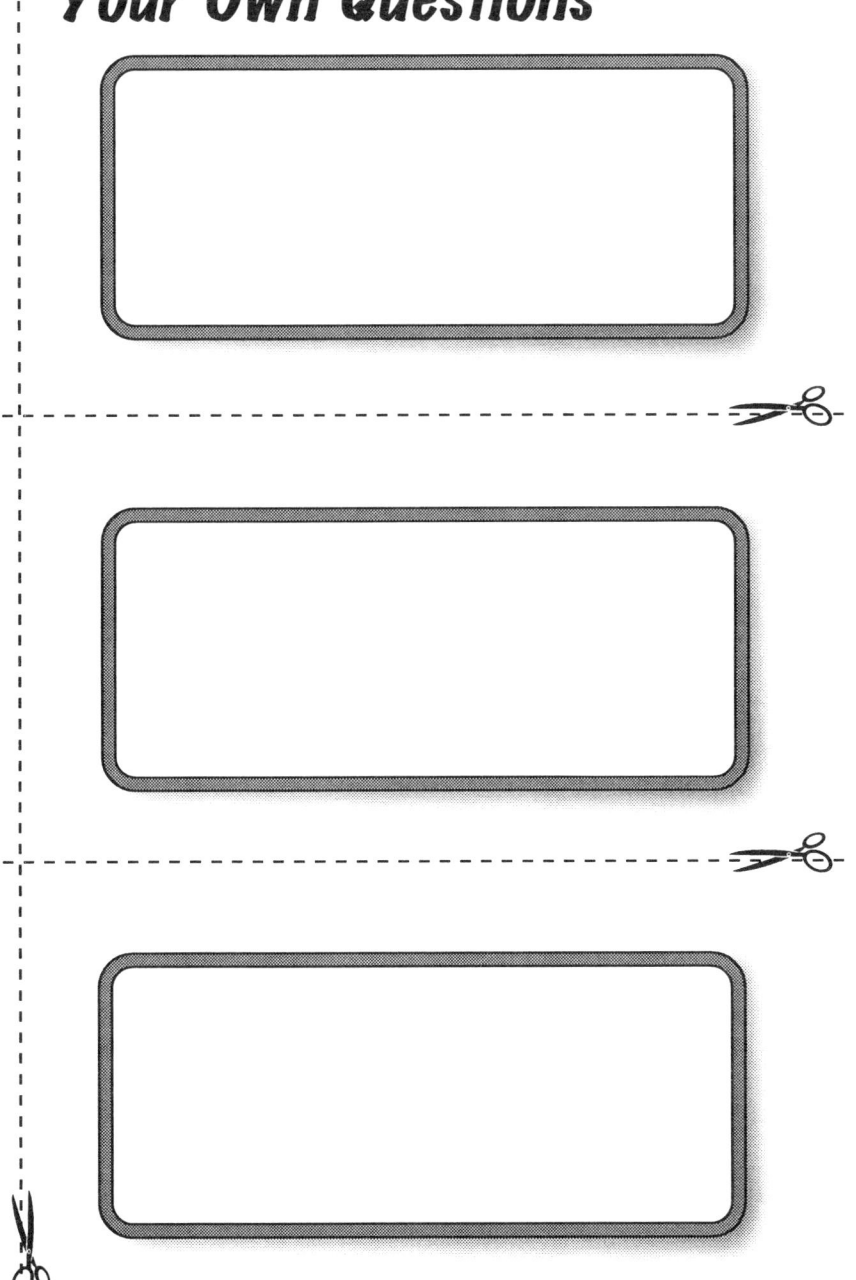

Correct Answers

Blank Cards for
Your Own Questions

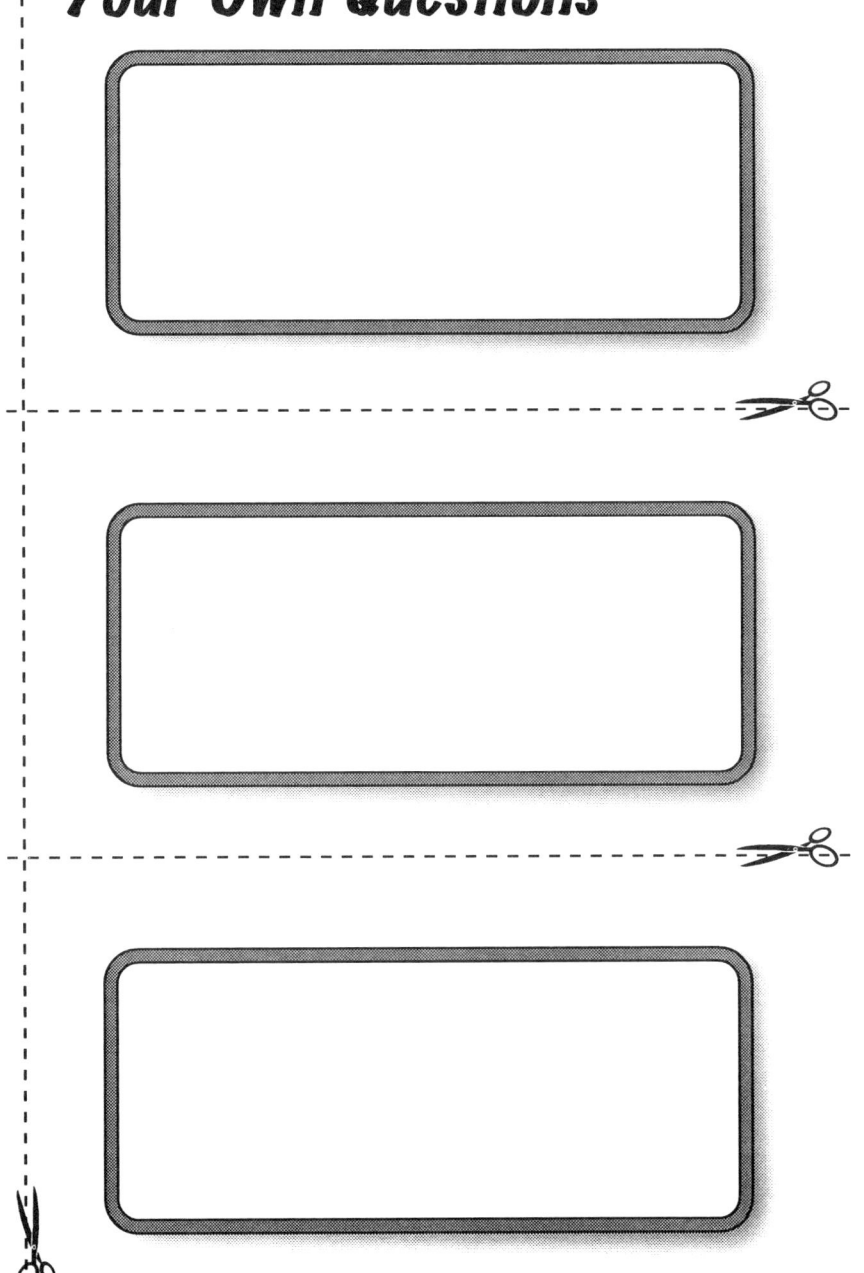

Correct Answers

Blank Cards for *Your Own Questions*

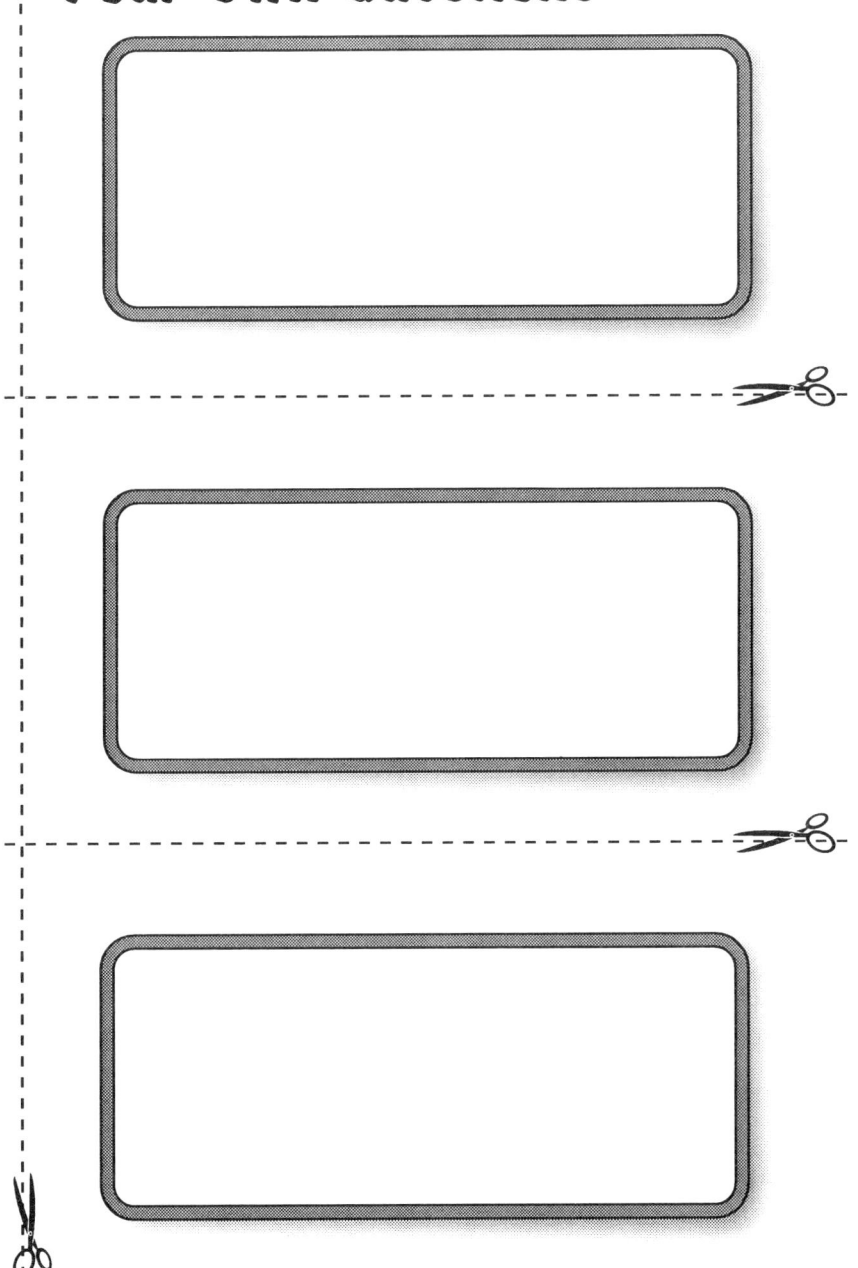

Correct Answers

Blank Cards for
Your Own Questions

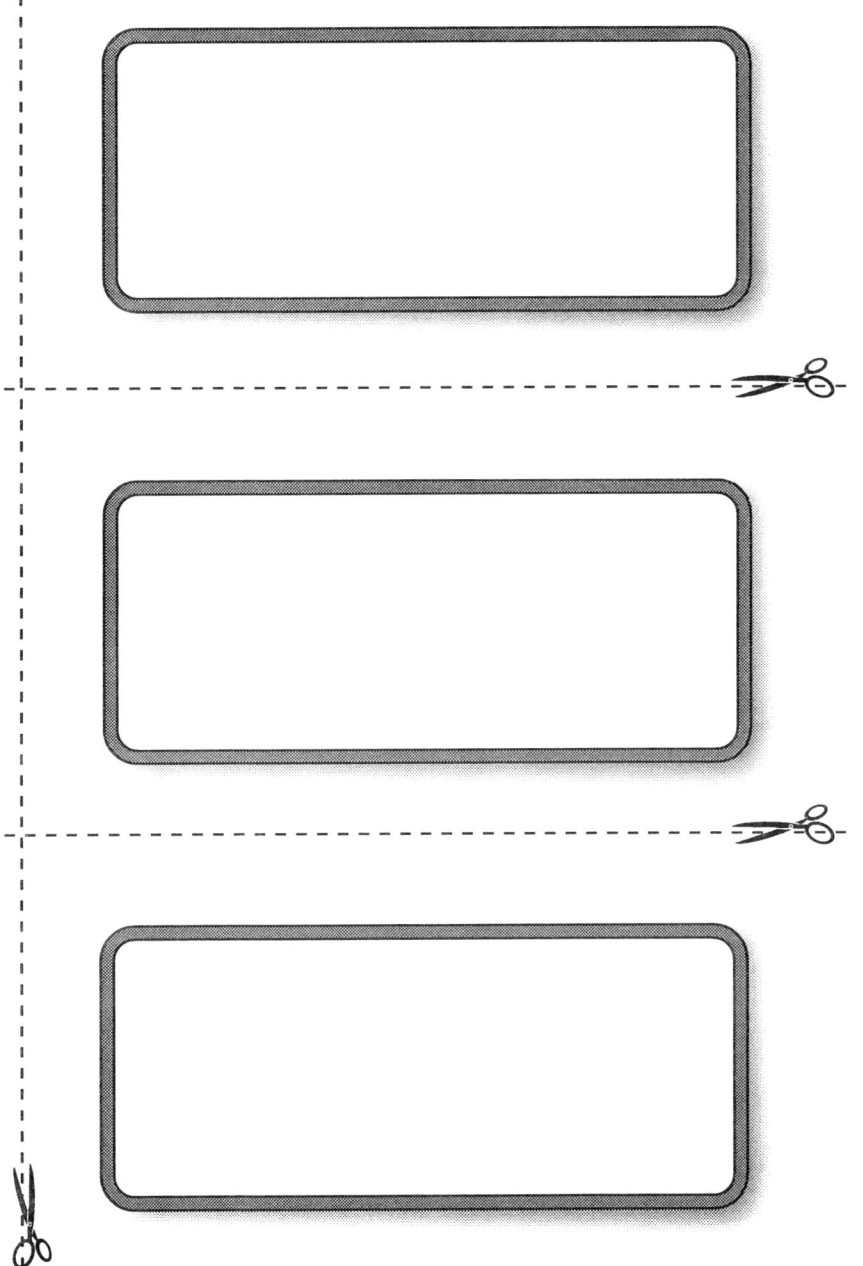

Correct Answers

Blank Cards for
Your Own Questions

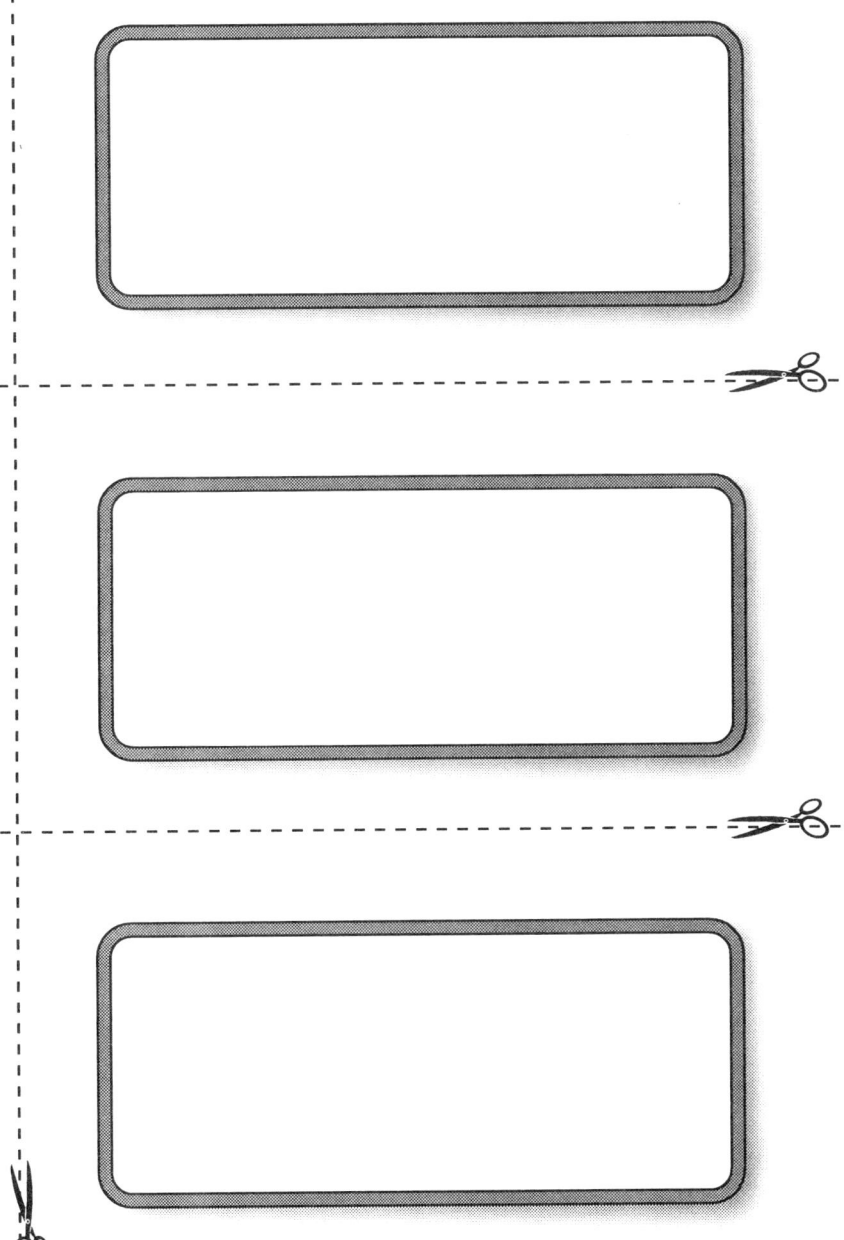

Correct Answers

Blank Cards for *Your Own Questions*

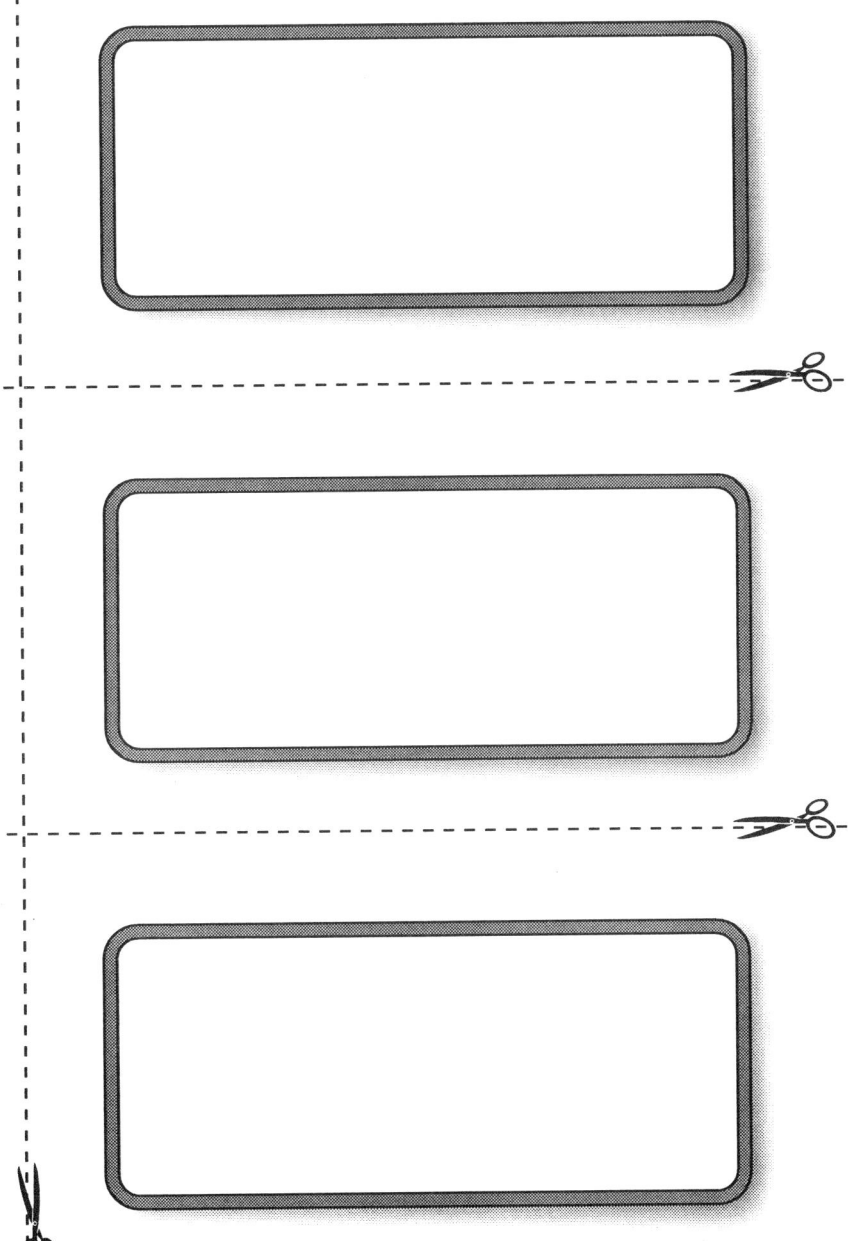

Correct Answers

Blank Cards for
Your Own Questions

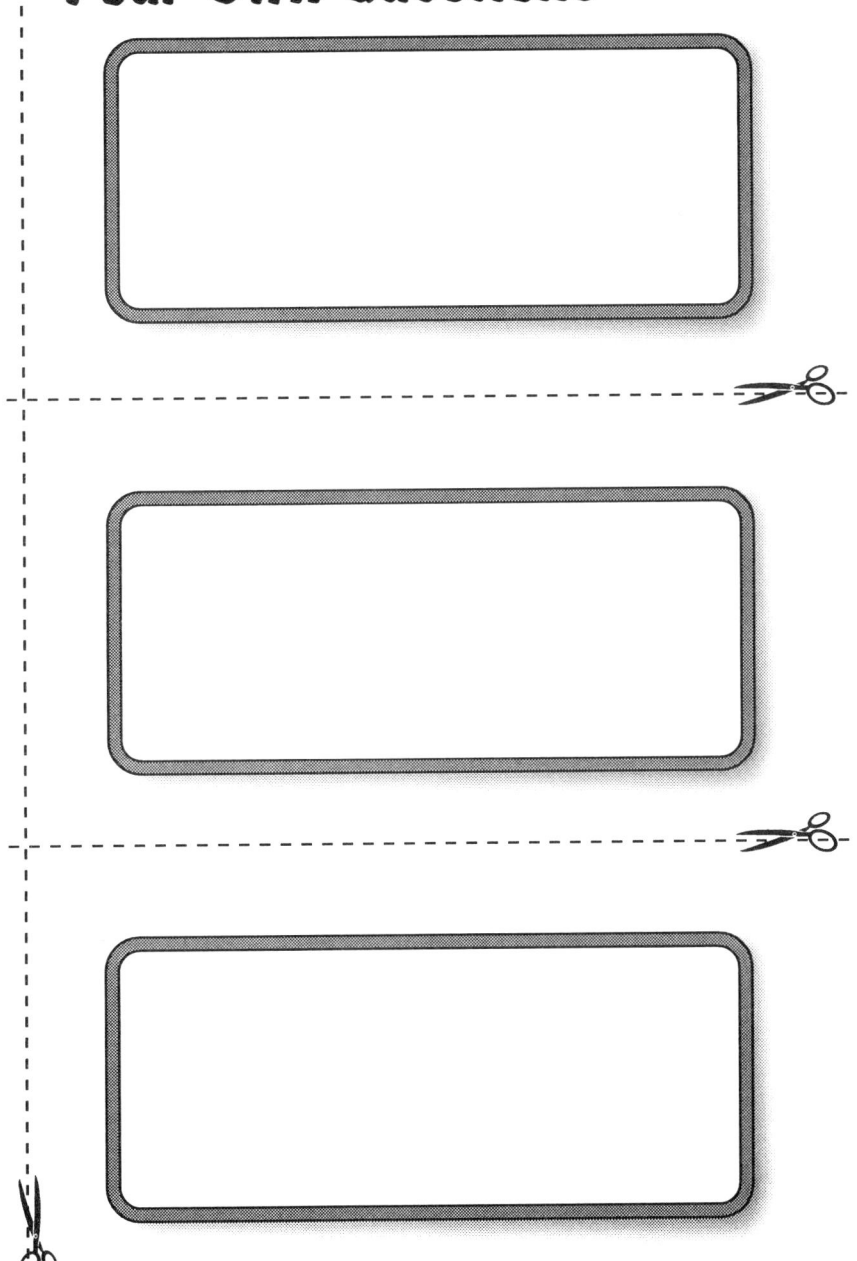

Correct Answers

INDEX

Clauses 612-618

Comparisons 823-831

Conditional Tense 849-860

Demonstrative Adjectives and Pronouns 790-805

Future Tense 838-848

General Questions/Verbs 861-864

Gustar 342-345

Imperatives: Formal Direct Commands 133-204

Imperatives: Informal Direct Commands 61-132

Imperfect Forms 249-276

Indefinite Expressions 467-500

Infinitive, Gerund and Present Participle 437-466

Past Participle 522-550, 884-897, 988-990

Past Subjunctive Forms 1-42, 954-960

Past Subjunctive Versus Present Subjunctive 43-60

Possessive Adjectives and Pronouns 501-521

Practice Command Forms 205-220

Prepositions 806-822, 980-984

Present Participle 870-883, 985-987

Preterite Forms 221-248

Pronouns 364-404, 551-595, 770-789, 971-979

Review/Verb Forms 280-341, 596-606, 619-708, 733-769, 898-903, 961-970

Ser, Estar 405-436

Synonyms 730-732

Translation/Vocabularly 277-279, 609-612, 709-729, 832-837, 904-946

"The ESSENTIALS" of LANGUAGE

Each book in the LANGUAGE ESSENTIALS series offers all the essential information of the grammar and vocabulary of the language it covers. They include conjugations, irregular verb forms, and sentence structure, and are designed to help students in preparing for exams and doing homework. The LANGUAGE ESSENTIALS are excellent supplements to any class text or course of study.

The LANGUAGE ESSENTIALS are complete and concise, with quick access to needed information. They also provide a handy reference source at all times. The LANGUAGE ESSENTIALS are prepared with REA's customary concern for high professional quality and student needs.

Available Titles Include:

French   *Italian*

German   *Spanish*

If you would like more information about any of these books, complete the coupon below and return it to us or visit your local bookstore.

RESEARCH & EDUCATION ASSOCIATION
61 Ethel Road W. • Piscataway, New Jersey 08854
Phone: (732) 819-8880

Please send me more information about your LANGUAGE **Essentials books**

Name _____

Address _____

City _____ State _____ Zip _____